THAT GRIM RED DAWN

SHETLAND'S SACRIFICE
AT THE ANCRE

by Jon Sandison

Best Wishes to Gary.

Jon Sandison

Cover shows Gordon Highlanders moving up to the forward
area on the Albert - Bapaume road, near La Boisselle, July 1916.
Photo courtesy: Imperial War Museum

I.S.B.N. 978-0-0905924-63-2
E.A.N. 97800905924632

Funded by the Scottish Government's Public Library Improvement Fund

Published by Shetland Library

Lerwick, Shetland
2018

CONTENTS

La a'Blair s'math n Cairdean

(It is good to have friends on the day of battle)

The *Shetland News*, 30th November, 1916

Friday, the 24th inst, will not be forgotten in Shetland for many a long day. The post which was delivered that day brought the saddest tidings which have ever come to the town. Swiftly it became known, as the dread news leaked out and passed from lip to lip, that the Shetland Territorials had suffered very heavily in the great Battle of the Ancre in France.

FOREWORD

One hundred years after the end of the First World War, it is still difficult to make complete sense of the impulse that drove thousands of young men from across Britain to don uniforms and march off to distant battlefields. Most were regulars or conscripts, some were part-time soldiers of the Territorial Force, but for the most part they were volunteers answering the appeal of Lord Kitchener, Secretary for War, who on 8 August 1914 called for 100,000 volunteers aged between 18 and 30, the aim being to create an army of approximately 1.2 million men by 1917.

Within a month that figure had been reached and by the end of October there were sufficient men to form 15 new divisions. One day that month 35,000 men enlisted, as many as had been recruited during the whole of 1913. In Scotland, as in other parts of the country, the call to arms was shrill and insistent. 'I feel certain that Scotsmen have only to know that the country urgently needs their services to offer them with the same splendid patriotism as they have always shown in the past,' wrote Kitchener in a letter which was given considerable prominence in the Scottish press.

Several factors prompted those volunteers to take the King's Shilling. Workers doing repetitive or menial jobs saw a chance to escape the drudgery of their existence. Peer pressure was brought to bear on the undecided and there was a general feeling that the whole thing was a bit of a lark and that it would be a shame to miss the great adventure. In those days, too, words such as duty, honour and patriotism were not idle concepts but the cornerstone of many young lives. During this period soldiers of the Territorial Force were given the option to serve overseas and the majority of its part-time soldiers accepted, including every man in the Shetland Companies of the Gordon Highlanders. Few seem to have given any thought to the dangers that lay ahead or even that warfare would bring casualties.

It is against that background that over 1,600 men from Shetland served in the British Army between 1914 and 1919. More than 270 were killed in action; a savage percentage for a fragile island community. Of these, 22 were killed or fatally wounded on a single day, 13 November 1916, on the River Ancre during the final phase of the Battle of the Somme, and their fate provides a sombre leitmotif for the wider Shetland losses during the war. By retelling their stories Jon Sandison has done a huge service by reminding us that these are not dusty names on a war memorial but were once vibrant young men who left behind grieving families and parents denied the opportunity of seeing their sons become men.

Those who survived the war were promised 'a world fit for heroes'; those who were less fortunate were the 'glorious dead'; those whose bodies were never traced or were atomised in the monstrous slaughter were soldiers 'known unto God'. In this centenary year it is fitting that the world should pause and remember them and the events which shaped their lives, not just in a spirit of commemoration, but in a mood of contemplation and profound thankfulness.

Trevor Royle is a Member of the Scottish Government's Panel for the Commemoration of World War I and the author of **The Flowers of the Forest: Scotland and the First World War** *(Birlinn).*

INTRODUCTION

I heard a lot about the Battle of the Ancre when growing up in Lerwick. But, it was not something ingrained in our local history. My father reminded my brothers and I it was at the Ancre that Shetland endured a huge loss of men during the Great War.

Little was written or mentioned about this local loss of life, apart from a reference in the Shetland Roll of Honour and Service:-

This heavy list of casualties came as a great shock to Lerwick, where every one of the killed and wounded was intimately known, and where, in the case of the killed, the loss was regarded more as a personal than a national one ... Shetland soldiers (Territorials) made their greatest sacrifice in any one battle at Beaumont-Hamel, in the storming of which the Highland Division earned undying fame.[1]

There is also reference to the Ancre in the inspirational work by the late Alex Cluness on Robert Greig. He mentions that the date marks *one of the saddest days in the history of Shetland in the Twentieth Century.*[2] His grandfather, Lance Corporal Alexander Cluness, was there.

Our local history is rich and varied, but I was astounded that little was known about this battle which impacted on our community so much.

My Grandad was also a local Territorial Gordon Highlander, and most probably at the Ancre. Like most, little was said about his war. Constantly seeing a photograph on the wall of a Grandad whom I never knew, in kilted uniform, resulted in a constant urge find out more about his war and the Ancre. In seeking the story

---

1   *Shetland's Roll of Honour and Service*, ed., Thomas Manson (T. & J. Manson, Shetland News Offices) 1920. p.270-1.
2   Greig, R.M., ed., Alex Cluness, *Doing His Bit. A Shetland Soldier in the Great War* (Shetland Times), 1999, p.x.

of him, it inevitably became a story of larger proportions, and therefore the story of them all.

It was through this battle the collective catastrophic devastation of war drifted back to home. At the same time it is understandable that the story is not mentioned much in Shetland history books. In a month, mostly on one day, 22 local men died due to action. A loss of a bairn is more than can be borne for any family; the list of casualties included only sons who never came home. The Ancre was when the impact of the Somme hit Shetland. Amongst the lost, a swimmer, footballers, a photographer, an ornithologist, a teacher, and a drummer in the Lerwick Brass Band. So much achieved in their short lives, yet much more to give. All brave in their own ways, some demonstrated extreme bravery.

This book is a testimony to the memory all of the men who fought in this battle, their families who had to bear their loss, or scarred state physical or mental upon return. It should act as a permanent reminder to our community as to why the Ancre should never be forgotten in our history.

This story will focus on why this battle was fought, the local men who fought in it, and the wider impact on our community. It is also a reminder that the battlefields on the Western Front and elsewhere where they, and all the others fought, is part of our own local heritage; places every Shetlander should visit.

The men today are a photo and a distant memory. Thankfully, their memories have not been forgotten during the 100th anniversary of the Great War. Ideally there should be more accurate information as to where each was at a particular time during the battle. However, with the loss of individual soldier records during the Blitz, there is little information available. In regimental War Diaries, only the loss of the odd officer tended to be recorded, with little mention of lower ranks.

Perhaps the biggest mistake and regret, understandably given what they experienced, is that that more could not have been gleaned about these special men while they were here. If there is one lesson for us all, it is write down all we can *because for your tomorrows these gave their today*.[3] There were many reasons for veterans to remain silent given the trauma they experienced, often encapsulated by a powerful self-censorship, designed to protect those at home from the worries they went through.[4] Cluness, emotively expounded on the passing of this generation in 1999 commenting that *the time to learn from the boys of the trenches has all but gone. History repeatedly delivers the same harsh lesson:- ask before it's too late*.[5]

Yet, thanks to the pages of our local newspapers, and relatives of those involved, some individual stories can be told. These accounts begin to let us know a little bit about a person, a loved one, a son, a brother or a friend.

3   Paraphrase of Epitaph, *because for your tomorrows these gave their today,* by John Maxwell Edmonds, 1944.
4   Whittingham, D., *Mud in The Great War:- Myth and Memory* (Hambledon) 2005, p.9-10.
5   Greig, R.M., ed., Alex Cluness, *Doing His Bit. A Shetland Soldier in the Great War* (Shetland Times) 1999, p.xiv.

The Shetland Territorials marching to Victoria Pier on 13th June 1915, to embark on the troopship *Cambria*.

Photo courtesy: Shetland Museum and Archives

THE SHETLAND SOLDIER
1914-18

Casualties amongst Shetlanders in the Army increased each year, from 6 in 1914, an estimated 67 in 1915, to over 140 in 1916. It is estimated over 1,600 Shetland connected men served in land forces during 1914-18, some also part of the Royal Flying Corps, later Royal Air Force. There are various challenges about what defines a Shetlander - born in Shetland, two Shetland parents or just one, someone born outside Shetland, but with two or one Shetland parents? Or, perhaps someone with no connection other than the fact they worked here? Either way, it does not matter; all have Shetland connections; and were Shetland soldiers.

These men served in Scottish regiments such as the Gordon Highlanders, Seaforth Highlanders and Royal Scots, and wider British regiments such as the Royal Field Artillery, Royal Engineers and Northumberland Fusiliers. Large numbers having emigrated prior to the war, enlisted with the Australian, Canadian and New Zealand forces. Most were in the 21-30 age group. Losses peaked in 1917 at almost 170.[1]

Despite recruitment in Shetland being heavily influenced by links to the sea, the numbers involved in the army, for a remote island community are apparent. The Gordon Highlanders enlisted almost 400, being the official Territorial regiment with good travel links and communication in Aberdeenshire. The numbers were boosted by vibrant local Territorial Companies. These men were originally part-time soldiers, keen to do their bit. Reasons for joining up locally varied - an extra source of income, peer group or female pressure, unemployment, propaganda, fear of invasion, and patriotism.[2] Of 22 Shetland connected men

---

1   Shetland Service and Loss in the Army, First World War Data. Jon Sandison (Combined sources of Shetland Family History Society, Scotland's War Project, Shetland Museum and Archives and *The Shetland Roll of Honour and Service*, 1920, ed., T. Manson).

2   Riddell, Dr Linda, *Shetland and the Great War* (Edinburgh University) 2015, p.113.

Belmont cable guard, 1915.   Photo courtesy: Shetland Museum and Archives

killed in the battle, 19 were Gordons, mostly in the Shetland Companies Gordon Highlanders. The loss at the Ancre also gave indication of wider involvement in the battle, with others from the Royal Fusiliers' Sportsman Battalion, Royal Scots and Royal Army Medical Corps.

During 1914-15 one of the Shetland Territorials' first duties was to guard telecommunication cable landfalls throughout the islands. A photograph of the Belmont cable guard shows ten men in 1915. From that group, four were killed on the Somme, including three at the Ancre. One was wounded during the summer Somme offensive, and another wounded at the Ancre. A far cry from the previous time spent at tranquil Belmont at the tip of the British Isles.[3]

Corporal William Robertson reflected on movements around Lerwick at this time in his diary:-

---

3   Shetland Museum and Archives Photo 'Belmont Cable Guard'. SM00112.

Friday 12th March, *Bright, sunny & dry. On orderly duty. Medium sized parade. Making Light Duty men clean up road. On parade in the afternoon. Attacking Staney Hill.*[4]

After the Shetland Companies had fulfilled their initial local defence role by 1915, the army authorities contemplated how to effectively utilise such a small body of fully trained soldiers. Probably their role in a full-scale European war had not been considered. The Territorial Force was founded by the Liberal Secretary of State for War, Richard Burton Haldane, an integral element of a wider ranging series of army reforms including the provision of an effective expeditionary force and the means of its reinforcement.[5] From 1908 the four Territorial battalions of the regiment formed the Gordon Brigade of the Highland Division, but the Shetland Companies were attached as an individual small formation, although still administered in peacetime by the 4th Battalion at Aberdeen. It is likely the Shetland (Zetland) Territorial Association would have done all in its power to ensure the continued existence of the companies.

There was little if anything that such a small unit could be constructively used for other than for the "trickle drafting" process that did occur, with a mainland base in Banchory, Aberdeenshire.[6] Reflecting the same dynamics as 'Pals' battalions, by the autumn of 1914, the Territorial Force had its attractions too for men wishing to enlist with their friends in a local unit.[7]

On 13th August 1914, Lord Kitchener was keen to use Territorials to either reinforce the New Armies or to release regulars from overseas garrisons.[8] On 13th June 1915, over 200 of the Shetland Territorials left Shetland on s.s. *Cambria*. Many eventually signed up for Imperial Service, committing to service

4   Diary of William Robertson, Margaret Cooper.
5   Mitchinson, K.W., *England's Last Hope* (Palgrave Macmillan) 1988, p.1.
6   Charles Reid, Gordon Highlanders Museum, Research Enquiry Report. 44/16/cdr.
7   Simkins Peter, *Kitchener's Army. The Raising of The New Armies, 1914-16* (Manchester University Press) 1988, p.100.
8   Holmes Richard, *Tommy. The British Soldier On The Western Front* (Harper Collins Publishers), 2004. p.137.

Harold, William and Tom Sandison, at Scone, Perthshire.

Photograph courtesy: Jim Mainland

abroad. Originally 107 volunteered for foreign service and were in the 2/7th Gordons. The Gordons suffered heavily at Loos in 1915 and volunteers were wanted from the 2/7th battalion to reinforce the 7th Battalion front line men. The Shetland Company volunteered en-bloc. About half joined the Second Provisional Battalion at Fort Matilda, Greenock, employed on guard duties at shipyards and munition factories. These had not signed up for Imperial Service.

Those who volunteered included the twins William and Tom Sandison, and their first cousin Harold Sandison.[9] Alongside them was another William Andrew Sandison, my grandad. The lists of Territorials in the paper show William and William Andrew with their Territorial numbers opposite their names to save confusion.

William and Tom Sandison were the sons of Andrew and Catherine (Katie), Lerwick. William wrote to his mother, 21st September 1916:-

---

9   Sandison, Dr R., *A Family At War 1914-1918* (Shetland Life) November 1996.

From the very first day of mobilization I was enthusiastic about doing what I could in the war and tried in every way to get to France, till we did get away after fifteen months training. During all that time we were physically fit and were signed on for Imperial Service.[10]

Although conscription began in January 1916, it was the original part-time soldiers that were to form the bulk of those lost at the Ancre. Most were working in Lerwick or Scalloway occupations such coopers, bakers, office workers, shop assistants, joiners, or fresh out of school, often the academic Anderson Educational Institute. At least six month training should have been given to every Territorial battalion after mobilisation. Like other Territorial Battalions, given that the cohort contained men working in the same trades, this aided a sense of belonging and cohesion.[11]

Volunteers for overseas service landed in Thurso and entrained to Scone to join the 2/7th Reserve Battalion, for further intensive training prior to serving overseas. The two Williams, Tom and Harold were among them. About forty went to France at the end of 1915, and others early in 1916 to join predominantly the 1st, 4th and 7th Battalions, Gordon Highlanders, in the build up to the Somme in 1916.

The first draft left Southampton on the 3rd of December, and arrived in Etaples for training on the 12th. Some of these men were with their unit in the field by 21st January.[12] An internal record of the 1st Battalion, Part II Orders, 7th September 1916, lists 271 reinforcements also being diverted to the 1st Battalion which had suffered heavy casualties in the early Somme battles. This Battalion was part of the 3rd Division, 76th Brigade.[13]

10 Sandison, Dr R., *A Family At War 1914-1918* (Shetland Life) November 1996.
11 Mitchinson, William, *The Territorial Force at War, 1914-16* (Palgrave Macmillan) 2014, p.29.
12 Service Record of Lance Corporal William Sandison, National Archives, WO363
13 Charles Reid, Gordon Highlanders Museum, Research Enquiry Report, 44/16/cdr.

At Christmas in 1915, some Territorials wrote home:-

We are having a very quiet time here. The New Year didn't turn out anything great. We were allowed a little latitude on Hogmanay night, and the boys brought in New Year in good style, (with the aid "o" a drap of champagne). One chap insisted in kissing all and sundry in the billet, and I hope he enjoyed the three or four days growth of "whisker" which was conspicuous in a good many case.[14]

In another letter a Terrier said:-

I have got both your letters all right. It appears you have had rather a boisterous "track o' wadder" at Xmas time, and yet I see from the paper that there was a good bit of stir all the same. We were beginning to wonder what was keeping the Shetland mail so long, but that was explained when we saw you hadn't had a boat for nine days. A mail arrives here every day, and we were expecting something every day.[15]

Another wrote:-

We are not at camp now as in England, but are sleeping in fine warm barns, which are clean and healthy. We are not in the firing-line, but are digging trenches, which you will be pleased to hear is quite safe; but I don't think I am pleased.

There are about 20 Shetland boys here and the same number in the firing-line, and so far as we know none of them are hurt yet. Where we are working we can hear the guns plainly and sometimes see the shells bursting. It is interesting to see aeroplanes getting shelled. You can see the shells bursting all around them. There are aeroplanes flying all around us every day.[16]

---

14 *Shetland News*, 27th January, 1916.
15 *Shetland News*, 27th January, 1916.
16 *Shetland News*, 27th January, 1916.

SHETLAND ANCRE 'DIVISIONS'

The Battle of the Ancre, 13th November 1916, was the final phase of the Somme Offensive. It incorporated an attack on the German front line as it crossed the Ancre River. Here the first major concentrated loss of men for Shetland occurred, like so many other parts of Britain had endured during the summer on the Somme. The principal objective was to get rid of the German salient between the Albert-Bapaume road and Serre, with the village of Beaumont-Hamel at its head.

The Shetland youth engaged significantly on this front at two key locations. Many were Gordon Highlander Territorials serving in the 51st Highland Division. They were in the Division's 4th and 7th Battalions just south of Beaumont-Hamel, and in 1st Battalion, part of the 3rd Division, just to the north at Serre. A battalion at full strength was just over 1,000 officers and men. Around 800 would be involved in an attack, the remaining 200 being Head Quarters staff, medics, support troops and specialists. The 51st recruited from the crofting counties, along with Nairn, Moray, Banff, Aberdeenshire, Kincardineshire, Perthshire and Angus. Those men could be confident of joining up with friends, but ultimately tightly-knit communities like Shetland would mourn the loss of so many men folk in one action.

THE CLENCHED
FIST OF THE SOMME

The Somme offensive was planned late in 1915, as a joint French-British attack, intended date 1 August 1916. The German Verdun offensive put severe pressure on the French who demanded that the attack be brought forward to 1st July, in order to divert German resources. The new British Commander in Chief Sir Douglas Haig agreed, although he preferred an offensive among the open ground of Flanders. Later in the year the need to maintain pressure on the Germans in aid of Russian and Romanian offensives also influenced decision-making.

Four Shetlanders were killed on the first day, alongside over 19,000 British fatalities. For the Gordon Highlanders there had been a few casualties from the initial Territorial posting during the summer Somme offensive during Battle of High Wood. Lance Sergeant Harold Sandison lost his life there, shot by a sniper on the 2nd of August. A prominent member of the local Territorial grouping, he was the husband of Daisy Campbell. He was identified later by a coin marked with the initials 'H.S.', and a key-tag number certified by the British Key and Property Registry Ltd., issued to him in 1907. His loss must have hit the Territorials hard.[17] A family gravestone in the Lerwick Cemetery has his name on it.

From 14th-15th September General Sir Henry Rawlinson's British Fourth Army made repeated attempts to win Delville Wood and High Wood. It was also embroiled in a bitter contest for Guillemont and Ginchy, both of which were captured in the first half of September.[18] General Sir Hubert Gough's Reserve Army, assumed more prominence in the offensive. After a struggle starting 23rd July, troops of I ANZAC Corps had captured Pozieres by 5th August, as well as the ruined mill on next ridge line beyond the village. A large proportion of the British attacks from mid-July to early September were small-scale affairs, aiming to move the British line forward to win local tactical advantages and improve the starting position for mid-September. In a war dominated by artillery, it was vital to straighten the start line before a big assault so the preliminary bombardment and supporting barrage were as accurate as possible. The price was a deterioration of the BEF's combat strength.

A new major British assault on 15th September against the German third main position saw the first-ever use of tanks. Objectives for the Fourth Army that day included the German third position in front of Flers and the capture of Gueudecourt, Lesboeufs and Morval. The Canadian Corps, part of the Reserve Army, was to seize Courcelette. The British XV Corps helped

---

17 *Shetland Times*, 3rd November, 1928.
18 Simkins, P., *From The Somme to Victory* (Pen and Sword Books) 2014, p.102.

by four tanks, took Flers and High Wood. Martinpuich and Courcelette were also secured. Haig believed that the Germans on the Somme were close to collapse, and judged the battlefield skills of his own forces to be improving. Grinding down the Germans was important, as was continued pressure for the French.

The British army in France was now approaching its maximum strength in number, still developing in terms of tactics, technology, command and control. On the eve of the Ancre, it could be viewed as being a far more effective instrument of war than it had been in July. Despite the long months of the Somme, British morale remained good, but with the enthusiasm of the summer substituted by a dogged determination.[19]

Men of the New Army and the greatly expanded Territorial battalions alongside those from the varied corners of the British Empire were positive. Most of these men, like those from Shetland, had been civilians - they had marched, drilled and mastered the basic skills of soldering. Developments were taking place in artillery intensity, but still much had to be grasped by Haig, Rawlinson and Gough. Against this strategic and tactical background the focus of operations shifted partly back to the sector immediately north and south of the Ancre. Up until early November, there were over 60 Shetland connected casualties during the Battle of the Somme. These were spread across varied Regiments, including the Seaforth Highlanders, Northumberland Fusiliers, Canadian Infantry, Australian and New Zealand infantry.[20] To some, *'idealism perished on the Somme. The enthusiastic volunteers were enthusiastic no longer.'*[21]

19 Sheffield, G., *The Somme*, (Cassell Military Paperbacks) 2003, p.157.
20 Shetland Service and Loss in the Army, First World War Data. Jon Sandison (Combined sources of Shetland Family History Society, Scotland's War Project, Shetland Museum and Archives and *The Shetland Roll of Honour and Service*, ed. T. Manson).
21 Taylor, A.J.P., *The First World War* (Penguin) 1966, p.140.

Contemporary plan of the Battle of the Ancre.

Map courtesy: Imperial War Museum

THE BUILD UP TO THE ANCRE

Preparations began in early October. The provisional date for the joint attack was 12th October. The 51st, and many of the Shetland Territorials arrived in the Beaumont-Hamel sector in the middle of October 1916, and spent time wire cutting. As a rule, a battalion would put three companies into the front line, retaining the fourth as support.[22] The initial attack date was postponed due to the weather. The German line north of the Ancre had been strengthened by the German 12th Division, which, from 22nd October, took over the Beaumont-Hamel sector between the 52nd Division at Serre and the 38th Division at Beaucourt.

As the month wore on, rain turned the battlefield into a quagmire. Thick mud and mist added greatly to the problems of infantry and gunners. General Head Quarters was forced to alter its plans and delay Gough's operations on the Ancre. On 17th October, after Haig had consulted Gough and Rawlinson, it was agreed that instead of making a converging advance from both sides of the Ancre valley, the Reserve Army would attack astride the Ancre, possibly on 23rd October, with the Fourth Army's efforts to secure Le Transloy. On 21st October an important advance was made south of the Ancre on a front of 7000 yards securing all the high ground overlooking the river.[23] November saw continued rain and the weather remained mostly wet and stormy until on 3rd November. Haig authorised Gough to postpone the Ancre operations so long as arrangements were made to commence the assault without further delay as soon as the weather showed signs of becoming more settled. On the 9th the downpour at last stopped, the waterlogged ground hardening and freezing. Five days later Gough consulted with his corps commanders, and rated the prospects quite good. A success on the Ancre was desirable for the British High Command, not only to take pressure off British allies, but also because it would create a favourable impression at

22 Ross, Robert B., *The Fifty-First in France,* (Naval and Military History Press) 1918, p.61.
23 Cheyne, G.Y., *The Last Great Battle of the Somme, Beaumont-Hamel, 1916* (John Donald) 1988, p.v.

the inter-Allied military conference at Chantilly Haig was due to attend on 15-16th November.[24]

The brilliant storm of Beaumont-Hamel (Churchill's phrase)[25], has often been ignored in various accounts of the Somme. It was an important part of a series of battles collectively known as the Battles of the Somme. Since the offensive had begun, 50,000 British soldiers had perished, and nearly eight times that number had been wounded. During this time little had been achieved - objectives of first day were still in German hands, such as Serre, Grandcourt, Miraumont Ridge. At the same time German senior commanders had been aware for almost a month that preparations were being made to renew the assault in the northern flank of the British sector of the Somme. Weekly, the German army had observed the movement of reserves and increasing numbers of guns into the area. In early November there were artillery bombardments around dawn.[26]

When the offensive opened in July, the German line at Beaumont-Hamel ran where it had been established after the "Race to the Sea" in 1914. The site possessed great defensive advantages. The village, once some 160 houses grouped round a beautiful white church, had long since been reduced to rubble. The German front line consisted three to four lines of trenches over 1000 yards, more or less parallel to each other, inter-connected by communication trenches, each line having its own protective screen of barbed wire. Within the ruins were deep cellars the Germans had converted into secure dug outs, the entrances facing away from the British artillery and protected by barbed wire entanglements. Below the village lay many tunnels where men could shelter then move up for counter attack.[27]

The Shetland Territorials were waiting as part of the 153rd Brigade, and further north within the 3rd Division. They did so

24 Simkins, P., *From The Somme to Victory* (Pen and Sword Books) 2014), p.107.
25 Churchill, Winston S., *The World Crisis*, Vol III, 1916-1918 (Bloomsbury, 1950), p.126.
26 Shelden, Jack, *The Germans At Beaumont-Hamel* (Pen & Sword Military) 2006, p.89.
27 Cheyne, G.Y., *The Last Great Battle of the Somme, Beaumont-Hamel, 1916* (John Donald) 1988, p.v.

on ground which was atrocious whilst enduring continuous heavy downpours. Monday 13th November would be zero hour, 5.45 a.m.

As the evening fell on Saturday 12th November, up to 60,000 infantrymen started to move towards their assembly areas across the Ancre valley.[28] There were six divisions and a brigade involved in the attack on 13th November, providing an estimated total of about 110,000 troops. In terms of infantry it would be about 76,000 men. Also many were in brigade or divisional reserve (some of whom may have been in action and others not), of those 10% normally left out of the battle in case of a total disaster, on leave, and courses.[29] The objective was the high ground, including two trenches called Munich and Frankfort[30] to the north east of the village. This ground had to be broken if the 51st were to take Beaumont-Hamel.

ATTACK

From north to south seven divisions would take part. The 51st Highland Division directly opposite Beaumont-Hamel, flanked on its left by the 2nd, 3rd [with Shetland Gordons] and 31st Divisions, and on its right by the 63rd [Royal Naval], 39th and 19th Divisions. The British First Army's attack on 13th November involved II Corps south of the Ancre looking to move the Germans from the remains of their front system between the Schwaben Redoubt and St Pierre Division and establish a line facing north-east, abreast of Beaucourt. The principal strike was to be delivered north of the Ancre by V Corps. Here from right to left, the 63rd, 51st, 2nd and 3rd Divisions were to assault the original German defences between Beaucourt and Serre which had resisted capture

28 Cheyne, G.Y., *The Last Great Battle of the Somme, Beaumont-Hamel, 1916* (John Donald) 1988, p.v

29 Derek Bird, Western Front Association, Northern Branch.

30 Frankfort Trench was marked on trench maps and referred in the Divisional Official History as such. But, confusingly there is now a 'Frankfurt Trench British Cemetery' near the location.

since 1st July. Shetland boys featured across these Divisions. The first objective of V Corps, in what was intended to be a three-stage operation, extended from Beaucourt station on the Ancre, up the Beaumont-Hamel valley and around the eastern edge of the village and then across Redan ridge and the slope in front of Serre. An average advance of 800 yards would be necessary to complete this stage; 600 to 1,000 yards on lay the second objective, which ran from the western edge of Beaucourt and along the eastern slope of Redan Ridge before bending around the eastern edge of Serre, where a defensive flank was to be formed. The third corps objective was Beaucourt, on the right, near the Ancre.

The 51st and 2nd's objectives included Munich Trench which, in July, had formed a line between the German front defences and their second position from Grandcourt to Puisieux. Frankfort Trench, the second and final objective of the 51st and 2nd Divisions on 13th November, was beyond Munich trench on the slope of Redan Ridge.[31] The artillery density of the attack was high, with 472 field guns and howitzers, 173 heavy guns and howitzers. To support V Corps, there was one field gun to every 13.5 yards and one heavy gun to every 31 yards of front. There had been one field gun to every 21 yards and one heavy gun to every 57 yards on 1st July, and one field gun per 10 yards and one heavy gun per 21 yards on 15th September.

The attack launched in damp and cold fog had mixed fortunes. On the II Corps front, the 39th Division and two battalions of the 19th Division took most of their initial objectives, including St Pierre Division at a cost of under 1,000 casualties. On the other side of the Ancre the 63rd [Royal Naval] Division had an intense fight for Beaucourt, but with the help of units from the 37th Division, finally secured the village the following morning. The 51st cleared the ruins of Beaumont-Hamel by the late afternoon of 13th November. Unable for the moment to push on to the next objective, 250 yards of Frankfort Trench overlooking the Beaucourt-Ancre valley, the Highlanders paused to consolidate their gains.

---

31 Simkins, P., *From The Somme to Victory* (Pen and Sword Books) 2014, p.109.

Further north the assault was generally less successful. On the left flank opposite Serre, the troops of the 76th Brigade [3rd Division], containing Shetland Gordons, were hampered by clinging mud, waist deep in places. Finding few gaps in the German wire, they were only able to enter the enemy trenches in small groups. Some of the men of the 8th Brigade also took part. The 3rd crossed the German support and reserve trenches to reach the first objective, Serre Trench, but they were isolated parties and inevitably overpowered. The British 2nd Division, between the 3rd and the 51st, attacked the German positions along Redan Ridge. Its 5th Brigade arrived on schedule, at its own first objective Beaumont Trench, which stretched northward from Beaumont-Hamel, though the lead in troops suffered heavily from rifle and machine gun fire. The 6th Brigade on the left, soon ran into difficulties, especially around the Quadrilateral.[32] Mud, intact German wire and crossfire from German machine guns all impeded progress.

SERRE

The Serre sector had been comparatively quiet until 13th November. The 3rd Division took an allocated section of the front in preparation for battle. Amongst them were Shetlanders who served with the 1st Battalion Gordon Highlanders. Prior to attacking the Shetland men undertook musketry and bombing practice, and also a church parade, a last chance to think - and pray. They moved to assembly trenches, taking up positions on the evening of the 12th after a long hard march. At Zero Hour, the Division attacked; the 76th Brigade was on the left, the 8th Brigade on the right; the 9th Brigade was behind in reserve. The Regimental History stated, '*The 3rd Division had a hard task ahead of it.*'[33]

32 Quadrilateral: German trenches were so well constructed by deep dugouts that they considered the whole line impregnable, except for a section which jutted out into No Man's Land which they called *Heidenkopf* and the British called 'the Quadrilateral'.
33 Falls, Cyril, *Life of a Regiment, Vol IV, Official History of the Gordon Highlanders* (Aberdeen University Press) 1958, p.111.

The barrage began on 11th November, using more guns than 1st July. It targeted barbed wire, dugouts, and German positions. On 13th November, at 5.45 a.m., the 1st Battalion moved out into No Man's Land, protected by heavy fog as men lay down in the mud. Visibility stretched little more than a few feet. This area had changed little since July. The Germans relying on barbed wire and machine guns, had rebuilt their defences.

On the left of the 51st, the 2nd Division stalled in mud, and lost the barrage, yet some men reached Frankfort Trench before retiring to Beaumont Trench to consolidate. The division was not in touch with the 51st's left. On 2nd Division's left 3rd Division's assault was a disaster. It got bogged in the mud, the gaps in the German wire were few, while the following battalions got confused with the leading battalions, and the infantry lost the barrage. Some fought their way to the fourth objective [Green Line], but all were driven back or wiped out. By the end of the day the 3rd Division was back on its start line.[34]

Moving forward, those attacking encountered rotting corpses from the 1st July. Heavy rain transformed the ground into a quagmire, making advance difficult. By 9.00 a.m. those advancing were unable to break through the barbed wire and machine guns. Heavy mist made communication and co-ordination difficult.

On the right of the line, the 10th Royal Welch Fusiliers and 1st Gordon Highlanders got as far as the German fourth line, while on the left the 13th East Yorkshires [92nd Brigade] progressed as far as the third line before being shelled-out in friendly fire. Some remained at isolated points during daylight, large numbers returning after 7.00 p.m. Orders to halt the attack were dispatched at 5.00 p.m. One isolated party of the battalion did hold on in the German front line until dusk, but left under orders. Some men of the 1st Gordons reached the third line. The divisional artillery, unaware that any troops remained so far forward, dropped its barrage on them.

---

34 Campbell C., *Engine of Destruction* (Argyll Publishing) 2013. p.105.

It was a doleful day for the 3rd. Some progress had been made by the 2nd, but the two most northerly divisions the 3rd and the 31st were unable to hold on to what little ground they had gained - at a fearful price. They were now back in their starting off trenches. Serre, an objective for the 1st of July, was never taken. The attack renewed the next day. On 21st of February 1917 a patrol of the 21st Manchesters discovered that the Germans evacuated the village as part of their withdrawal to the Hindenburg Line. The 1st Battalion casualties that day came to 141 including eight from Shetland killed, plus two others from other regiments.

Private David William Anderson was a typical young high achiever with determination, and many interests. He was son of Laurence and Mary, Hoolsgarth, Lerwick, the eldest of five children.[35] Before the war, David was an apprentice at the North of Scotland Co.'s office where *'the utmost confidence and trust were placed in him by his employers, while he was very popular with all his fellow-workers and also with the public.'* David was always *'full of energy and enthusiasm'*, and before he was 10 years old, he had joined the Boys' Brigade, within which he was *'an energetic member for several years.'* He was a *'keen footballer and swimmer'*. Before he was 16 he was one of four Lerwick boys who swam Bressay Sound. As soon as he was old enough, he had volunteered for foreign service since he often felt *'it was his duty to go to the front where so many of his comrades were suffering all the horrors of modern war for him and others'*. He left for France in August of 1916, and had only been 3½ months on French soil before being killed.[36] David had been a member of the Sandwick cable guard upon the outbreak of war.

35 Shetland Family History Society.
36 *Shetland News*, 29th March, 1917.

The family received a letter from the British Red Cross:-

...Pte Cluness, Gordons, now in hospital abroad, and only to be reached by a letter, has no first-hand knowledge, but heard from two Shetland machine gunners Pte C Sinclair and Pte J W Johnson, of the Gordons, that they were in a shell hole when the Germans came up on each side of them.

One of the bombers then appeared and went to try and drive the Germans back, but he was hit by a sniper, and they saw him fall flat on his face. The two got back, and when they found that Pte Anderson was missing, they felt perfectly certain that he was the bomber they had seen.

... I think myself there can be no doubt that this was your son whom they saw, and that he fell in a brave attempt to drive back the enemy.[37]

Corporal William Robertson
Source: Manson 1920

A memorial inscription to David is found in Lerwick Cemetery, on the headstone for his mother and father. He is buried at Queens Cemetery, Puisieux. In this small cemetery west of Serre, two other Shetlanders rest near him, together just as they were in November 1916; **Corporal William Robertson**, aged 21, from Sullom, Northmavine, and **Corporal Laurence Bain Mackay,** aged 22, of 57 Commercial Street, Lerwick.

William joined the Territorials in 1911. He was the eldest of 4 children, son of James and Ursula. He and David were former pupils of the Anderson Educational Institute.

At school it was noted that William '*showed considerable talent in all subjects he took, and had passed examinations with distinction. But for the war he would have passed the higher Leaving Certificate examination in 1915, and then entered*

---

37 British Red Cross and Order of St John Letter to Mr L Anderson, Hoolsgarth, Albany Street. 21st April, 1917.

the profession he had chosen, which he had so earnestly and successfully studied for.' What the profession was is unknown.[38]

Laurence was the son of George and Jean Mackay and was brother to George (Dodie) Mackay, also a Sergeant in the Territorials. Dodie was a Lerwick postman after the war, and known as 'Cook Mackay'; the cook in the Shetland Territorial grouping. Laurence had been briefly home on leave in the autumn of 1916. A cooper by trade, it was noted that *'he was among the tallest of the Gordons, and his bravery was equalled by the gentleness and kindness of disposition. It is no figure of speech to say that he was a great favourite with all who knew him and the most genuine sympathy is felt for his widowed mother who mourns a loving and devoted son.'*[39]

Standing in this small, personal cemetery today, all 3 headstones can be seen from the gate.

Also killed in this sector was **William Henry Leask Johnston,** son of Thomas and Andrina, North Roadside, Lerwick, aged 20. A local Territorial, he had been in France with one of the early Gordon drafts. Prior to the outbreak of war, he had been an apprentice joiner with Mr M.P. Morrison. He was also a former A.E.I. pupil.

A comrade, Private John Cowie, sent this letter to his widowed mother:-

I am sorry to tell you that Willie was killed in action in the big advance, which I suppose you have heard of by now. I was beside him at the time, when a shell came over and a piece caught him in the head, and the same shell wounded another four of our mates. It will be a relief to you to know that he suffered no pain, but died about ten minutes after he was struck. We carried him a few miles behind the firing line, and gave him a decent burial. This will be a very hard blow to

---

38 *Shetland News*, 14th December, 1916.
39 *Shetland Times*, 9th December, 1916.

you, but it has been the same to me, as Willie has been my chum since he came to this Battalion, and was a nice, cheery boy, and the whole Pioneer section wish to sympathise with you in your bereavement.[40]

William is buried at Euston Road Cemetery, Colincamps.

William Gilbert Manson, also an A.E.I pupil, aged 20, died of wounds on the 1st of January, 1917, aged 20. He was the elder son of William Spence Manson, boot and shoe maker, and Eliza, of 33 Commercial Road, Lerwick.[41] Despite his wounds, letters received from the hospital showed very good progress.

The report mentioned that William was an *admirable patient, and it was hoped that this, together with his cheerfulness, would have pulled him through.* He is buried at Boulogne Eastern Cemetery.

Sister E. Brown, a member of staff at the hospital, sent a letter to his father:-

I do not know how to write such sad news to you. I have not written to you for a few days because your son was not so well, but I thought it was only temporary, as he had so many ups and downs, and I was hoping to send you good news. However, this morning he got suddenly worse and died unexpectedly. I am sure this will be a great shock to you all, as I have been sending hopeful news lately, but one could not forsee what would happen. We are all very upset about him, as we had nursed him through two critical periods. I can assure you that everything possible was done for him, and I only wish it could have been to good effect. Please accept my deepest sympathy in your great sorrow.

The Chaplain wrote to Mr Manson in the following terms;-

---

40 *Shetland News*, 30th November, 1916.
41 *Shetland News*, 23rd November, 1916.

I am more sorry than words can express to let you know that your dear son passed away today quite unexpectedly. He suddenly turned worse, and heart failure ensued. We are all deeply grieved about his death because we were all devoted to him. The doctors and nurses could not possibly have been kinder and more attentive than they were, and we all hoped he would pull through. What a splendid patient he was! So brave and uncomplaining, and he liked so much when I prayed with him. We were all greatly struck also by his love of home and his devotion to yourself. He wanted to get better that he might show you how much he loved you and appreciated all you have done for him. Your dear son will be laid to rest in a beautiful cemetery here, by the side of other brave comrades who have also laid down their lives for our own sake.

The *Shetland News* expressed its deep sympathy for Mr Manson, *who has had a very anxious time since his son was wounded, and who has now to bear the greater sorrow which comes to him upon his death.*[42]

He is buried at Boulogne Eastern Cemetery, Boulogne.

Gilbert Brown aged 21, son of Gilbert and Margaret, originally of Sullom, was killed.[43] He was a cooper at the Messrs. Slaters' barrel factory in Lerwick. The *Shetland Times* noted five months later that he had been *reported wounded and missing,* but *has now been reported killed on that date.* He joined the Territorials at 16 and had been in France since July of 1916.[44] His name is on the Thiepval Memorial.

Corporal William Hughson, aged 28, was the son of John and Barbara, 7 Union Street, Lerwick. He joined the Territorials

---

42 *Shetland News*, 11th January, 1917.
43 Shetland Family History Society.
44 *Shetland Times*, 7th April, 1917.

after the outbreak of war and was among the original active service men during their training in Scotland, where he gained his stripes. The *Shetland Times* added that he was *a prime favourite among the young people of the town, by whom his death will be much regretted* ... His father worked as a general labourer and both parents came from Skerries. William had been a member of the Viking Football team. The paper said his death brings up to six the number of Lerwick footballers who fell in the Battle of the Ancre :- *worthily have these gallant boys acquitted themselves in the greatest of all fields.*[45] His father and mother had died prior to the First World War. He is buried at Serre Road Cemetery, Number 1.

Arthur McCarthy, aged 23, born in Ireland, and came to Shetland from Liverpool, also died from wounds received in action on 16th November. The son of John and Margaret, he had worked for two years in the Custom House as a preventive officer. In Lerwick he joined the Territorials and was called up on the outbreak of hostilities. The *Shetland Times* noted *his sterling qualities had won him the esteem of a wide circle in Lerwick, who sincerely regret his death, and extend to his sorrowing parents and relations profound sympathy.*[46] He had only been one month in France. Arthur is buried at Varennes Military Cemetery.

Also killed near Serre as part of the 8th Brigade, 3rd Division, was **Private Robert William Inkster,** Lewis Gun Section, 2nd Battalion Royal Scots. Shetland links with Leith meant that after the Gordons and Seaforths, most Shetland connected men served with the Royal Scots. He was aged 27, and the son of John and Margaret. His father was a

Source: Manson 1920

fisherman from Burra where Robert had been

45 *Shetland Times*, 2nd December, 1916.
46 *Shetland Times*, 7th April, 1917.

born. Robert left Shetland with his mother and siblings at the turn of the century after his father was lost at sea. They stayed at 15 Forth Street, Grangemouth. His younger brother Thomas, 25, died just one month before of dysentery in Salonika. He served with the 10th Battalion Black Watch. Robert enlisted at Stirling on 8th December 1915, while employed as a clerk in the shipping office of his uncle, Mr Thomas Inkster. He joined the 2nd Royal Scots on the 29th of March 1916 and arriving in France on 22nd September, 1916.[47]

On the 12th, 'A' Company moved into the line at 8.00 a.m. and took over the assembly position from the 9th Brigade, with other Companies moved at 12.15 p.m. and halting at Courcelles for tea. The Battalion arrived in the trenches at 9.15 p.m.

On the morning of the 13th, the Battalion formed up with the 3rd Royal Scots on their right, marching into assembly position in front of Rob Roy Trench at 5.00 a.m. At Zero Hour, the intense bombardment began and continued for five minutes. During this time the assembly line ('A' and 'B' Companies) crossed the German front line with little opposition and penetrated the German second line where they were held up by uncut wire behind the parapets.[48] All dugouts in the front and second line were bombed. "Bombs" was the term used by the British at the time for grenades. A bombing team contained several men with various roles, intended to purge trenches and dugouts of their human occupants.

Similar to the fate of the Gordon Highlanders just further north, the attack failed, being unable to hold on the German line in thick fog and mud. For the rest of the 13th the German barrage was noted as being *exceptionally heavy*.[49]

Casualties in total were 274, two officers killed, 9 wounded and one missing. 19 other ranks were killed, 151 were wounded, 84 missing, 8 wounded and missing.[50]

---

47 *Shetland News*, 14th December, 1916.
48 The parapet formed the side of the trench directly facing the enemy line.
49 2nd Royal Scots Battalion War Diary. November 1916. National Archives WO 95/1423/3.
50 2nd Royal Scots Battalion War Diary. November 1916. National Archives WO 95/1423/3.

Robert's Battalion was relieved the following day.

A summary was written about Robert in the local press:-

In manner he was somewhat quiet and modest, but he had a very kindly, frank nature, which made him a great favourite among all with whom he came in contact, and those who knew him best speak most highly of him. He frequently came to Shetland for his holidays in pre-war days, when he stayed a short time with his relatives in the town, and renewed acquaintanceship with his old friends. Sincere sympathy is extended to Mrs Inkster, on whom the war has made a big sacrifice, for a younger son, Sergt Thomas Inkster, of the Black Watch, died in hospital at Salonika on 6th October, after only two days illness.[51]

Robert's name is also on the **Thiepval Memorial.**

The other Shetlander not in the Territorials killed this day was **Joseph Anderson**, aged 24. He was a son of Lerwick solicitor, John Bannatyne Anderson, and his wife Minnie. Joseph served a law apprenticeship in his father's office, followed by two years at Edinburgh University, qualifying in 1914 and returning to work with his father.[52] Not long after, he left Lerwick to join the Sportsman's Battalion of the Royal Fusiliers serving with the Second Division. They were in the line to the south of the 1st Gordon Highlanders.

A lengthy account of Joseph's death during the Ancre was given via a fellow soldier who had written home to his family. It was noted that he was one of the first Shetland casualties known about from the Battle.

In the morning of the 13th, we attacked in the front wave, the Boche was evidently taken by surprise, for we got into and over his front line without meeting much resistance, and with

---

51 *Shetland News*, 14th December, 1916.

52 Shetland Family History Society.

a few losses. Joe was one of the first few groups to reach the second line. He and his team came into immediate contact with a German machine gun which had just been brought up from its dug-out ... Joe fired and hit at least two of the Boche team before a shot from one of them struck him in the head and killed him instantly. It was a gallant piece of work, and Joe took a leading part in it. He certainly saved the life of No 1 of his gun, and many lives he must have saved too by leading the way in the destruction of a gun that would have had a heavy toll had it been allowed to get to business. The sympathies of many men in the Battalion who knew and admired Joe, and heard of and applauded his deed, go out to you in your bereavement. Most of all my own sympathies, for the loss is a very great one to me and that perhaps enables me to realise your loss and feel with you the more.

In addition to the soldier's message, it was mentioned that '*Pte Anderson, was a young man of much promise, and was most popular among all classes in the town. His cheerful friendly manner, his very marked good nature, and his generosity made him a general favourite. He was held in high esteem by young and old alike.*' [53]

He is buried at Canadian Cemetery No 2, Neuville St Vaast. He is commemorated on the A.E.I. Roll of Honour, Edinburgh University Roll of Honour, and St. Ringan's Church Roll of Honour

George Stout of the 93rd Field Ambulance, Royal Army Medical Corps was also killed north of Serre, aged 28, son of Robert and Tomima, Busta, Fair Isle. He left Fair Isle in 1909 to work as a taxidermist for Mr Charles Kirk, Edinburgh.[54] George volunteered there in 1914, and spent some time in Egypt from December 1915.[55]

---

53 *Shetland News*, 30th November, 1916.
54 *The Scottish Naturalist*, (Oliver & Boyd), No 61, January, 1917.
55 Shetland Family History Society.

George Stout
Source: Manson 1920

Dear Mr Stout, I wish to assure you of the deepest sympathy of all Officers and men of this unit in your great loss. Your son was one of the finest men it has been my fortune to meet. Besides being immensely popular, he had won the admiration of us all, and I can assure you that only the best and bravest can do that out here. I am not stating the usual condolences when I say he was probably the best man we had and the one among the men we could least afford to lose.

I was in charge of stretcher bearers, in the attack, which by now you will have read. Stout was put in charge of the party to take the wounded along the top of the trenches by trolley and just left me for a few minutes to complete his arrangements. I can still hear his last cheery "very good, Sir" as I left him, and I knew the job would be well done. A few minutes later shell landed in a party of them, wounding two others. It may console you to know his death was instantaneous, and he was not disfigured; two pieces struck him in the head and heart.

Thus died for his country, George Stout, whom I am proud to call a friend.

Yours sincerely,
R.S. Cumming, R.A.M.C., Captain.[56]

A memorial to George was published in the Scottish Naturalist, January 1917. It added that he was known to the readers and to many ornithologists *through the excellent work he accomplished as a bird-watcher in Fair Isle.*

The article went on:-

The writer became acquainted with him in Fair Isle in the autumn of 1905. George was then sixteen years old, and assisted his father, a crofter-fisherman. The subject of this notice was

---

56 Michelle Moggach (née Henderson) great grand niece of George Stout.

an enthusiastic devotee (of natural history), and only required the chance to become a skilled naturalist. His abilities were recognised and appreciated. He was supplied with books and binocular glasses, and these, together with a few weeks' training in the autumns of 1905 and 1906, equipped this apt pupil for the duties of bird-watcher at this now famous ornithological observatory - a post he filled with marked success.

The writer adds that, over the following years, George accompanied him to Fair Isle, St Kilda and Auskerry (Orkney), and the Butt of Lewis in 1914. *George became an accomplished field ornithologist, and well versed in the peculiarities of the flight and call-notes of migratory birds, especially those of rarer species...[57]*

He is buried at Couin British Cemetery.

57 *Scottish Naturalist* (Oliver & Boyd), No 61, January, 1917.

BEAUMONT-HAMEL

The 51st Highland Division arrived near Beaumont-Hamel in mid-October. They were commanded by Major-General Montague Harper, and had been involved in the failed attacks in July and August. Their insignia bore the letters 'HD' and the unit got nicknamed 'Harper's Duds'. After Beaumont-Hamel, this changed.

The ground that the Shetland men of the 7th and 4th Gordon Highlanders went over on the 13th of November had already seen much destruction and loss of life on 1st July. The Hawthorn Redoubt mine on the left hand side of the attack position had been blown. The 1st Essex Regiment at first found themselves unable to move because of heaped-up bodies of dead and dying in their trench. The Newfoundlanders were left to approach Y-Ravine on their own where some reached the German wire. In all, 710 became casualties. By the end of October, many German advantageous positions had been captured. But Beaumont-Hamel still posed a serious threat to Haig's forces. Possession of the fortress would provide a good jumping-off base when the offensive was renewed in the spring. A fresh mine shaft was dug towards Hawthorn Crater.[58]

The 51st was at the very middle of the five-mile long front to be attacked. It was in a favoured position for the formidable task of taking the village of Beaumont-Hamel via Y-Ravine. South of the village, as described in the previous chapter, lay Y-Ravine, menacing any direct approach from that quarter. Every morning from the end of October an intense barrage dropped on the front line German trenches.

The 51st Division, 153rd Brigade, with the Shetland men among them, took four hours to cover two and a half miles. Wet, and heavily laden with kit and equipment, both brigades set out at 9.00 p.m. on 12th November to march five miles from Forceville to the assembly trenches, relieved only slightly by a

---

58 Cheyne, G.Y., *The Last Great Battle of the Somme, Beaumont-Hamel, 1916* (John Donald) 1988, p.v.

The Battle of Ancre Heights 10-11th November. A general view of the remains of the ruined village of Beaumont-Hamel seen on 26th November 1916 after its capture. The heap in the centre is the remains of the church.

Photo courtesy: Imperial War Museum

45 minute stop between Mailly-Maillet and Auchonvillers for tea. Their compatriots in the 152nd Brigade, with twice as far to march, halted halfway for food and mugs of tea. At the same time, flares, light pistols, cartridges, and phosphorous bombs were distributed amongst the different platoons. An extra breakfast ration was provided consisting of tinned herrings or sausages, which was appreciated by the men. A further ration of chewing gum and a packet of chocolate was given to each man.[59]

A Lerwick Gordon Highlander with the 4th Battalion, James Houston of Union Street, gave an account of this day in his diary. On the 11th he noted:-

There is word of a big advance coming off soon. Up in the trenches clearing away some of the mud out of them. Mud two feet deep in some places. Got back about midnight.

The following day he added:-

Had breakfast at 9 a.m. We got some whale oil to rub on our feet and legs to prevent frost bite & trench feet. The advance is going to start tomorrow.[60]

Their assembly trenches turned out to be uninhabitable. So they spent a bitter cold night lying in the open behind the parados, the rear-side of the trench.[61] They reached their destination with an hour to spare before Zero. During the night, a bank of raw fog came up from the valley of the Ancre.

Parties of the 7th Gordons crept out into No-Man's Land at zero minus ten minutes, taking whatever cover was available. Night patrols had established the barbed wire had been suitably

---

59 Campbell, C., *Engine of Destruction* (Argyll Publishing) 2013, p.99.

60 James Houston diary, courtesy of Martin Emslie.

61 Both the parados and the parapet (the side of the trench facing the enemy) were protected by two or three feet of sandbags. Soldiers were instructed to build the parados higher than the parapet so that the defenders were not outlined against the sky and therefore easy targets for snipers. The parados also protected soldiers in front-line trenches against those firing from the rear.

cut. Battalions moving forward encountered deep mud and sodden kilts as they moved towards the jumping position, many just reaching this less than two hours before zero hour. Men were instructed not to cough so the Germans would not be alerted. Water bottles had to be full in order to avoid the clunk of half-empty flasks on the march.

The Shetlanders' part in this battle was graphically described by a local soldier in the *Shetland News* last edition of 1916. The paper mentioned that the writer was a *'well known Lerwick boy'*, William Sandison stated that they lay down to wait *'through the long midnight and early morning hours.'*

There is little hope of describing adequately the scene, or of setting down with any degree of clarity, the events of that grim red dawn. We had heard, it is true, the term 'barrage', till the word had become a familiar one, but not one of us had formed the slightest conception of the awful reality. On the afternoon of November 12th. we got orders to strike our packs, and parade in Fighting Order 'as for going into Action'. (Fighting order consists of Great Coat with ends fastened up French fashion; haversack in place of pack; one hundred and twenty rounds of ammunition, and four Mills hand grenades, two in each greatcoat pocket). At 6 p.m. we were in the trenches and 'took over the line', and all who were not on sentry were crammed into dugouts in the support trench to await orders. We sat on floors and stairs, smoking greatly, with fitful spells of sleep, until 11.30 p.m. when tea and a ration of rum were served. After that 'get ready to move', and in single file we went out on top and threaded our way among shell-holes and scraps of barbed wire, in the flickering light of intermittent flares. The silence was deadly. Only the sharp nervous rat-tat of a Lewis machine gun, or the hiss of a late-burning Star Shell spluttering in the mud, and the subdued rattle of bayonet scabbard or rifle butt.[62]

---

62 Sandison, Dr R., *A Family At War 1914-1918* (Shetland Life) November 1996.

As well as the above, men took with them an iron ration and a day's ration, filled water bottle, two sandbags and a tin disc [a military ID tag] attached to their haversack. Every alternate man carried either a pick or shovel in the proportion of two shovels to one pick. Some also carried wire cutters.[63]

William Sandison added:-

Behind the parapets of our front line we lay down to wait through the long midnight and early morning hours. At about 4 a.m. our rest was disturbed by some half-dozen trench shells tearing and screaming at random for some troublesome gun emplacement and by the intermittent thundering of our own field guns; and the word was passed, 'We attack at 5.45 a.m.'[64]

Another Shetlander wrote to his brother-in-law John Gair. Lance Corporal **William David Arthur,** of Cuckron, Stromfirth, Weisdale wrote a letter describing this moment in a more sombre, yet upbeat fashion:

We duly arrived at the trenches, took up our positions, and awaited the dawn of morning which would see us hard at work. The night passed without any fresh event happening. Fritz being pretty quiet all the time, which was lucky for us for if he had started shelling it would have been pretty uncomfortable. About midnight we moved up to the front line, and there we lay until six in the morning. Everything was quiet, and at that time it was still pretty dark. We knew, however, that after waiting the long, weary night, that at last the hour had arrived. Then with a crash like thunder our artillery burst forth and the air whistled with shells. The ground shook as if by an earthquake. Then the charge sounded and over we went.[65]

---

63 7th Battalion Gordon Highlanders War Diary. WO 95/2882/1, National Archives.
64 Sandison, Dr R., *A Family At War 1914-1918* (Shetland Life) November 1996.
65 *Shetland News*, 21st December, 1916.

Arthur brothers, of Kurkigarth, Stromfirth. Willie Arthur (Gordon Highlanders), Jeemie Arthur (H.M.S. *Vanellus*). Photo courtesy: Shetland Museum and Archives

This moment in the battle was ominously summarised by the Division's historian:-

The most unimaginative loon, particularly if it is not his maiden fight knows that there are many men assembled with him who in an hour or two will see dawn break for the last time.[66]

The silence was broken when the attack took place with a pre-dawn bombardment. It was 4.00 a.m. when their rest was disturbed by around six 4-inch shells and by *'intermittent thundering of our field guns'*. By this stage, the word had passed that they attack at 5.45 a.m.[67]

At 5 a.m. messages were received from all company commanders that the men were lined up and ready to go.[68]

The barrage opened; a barrier of fire from artillery which was to act as a shield for men advancing. At the same time, the Hawthorn Crater mine erupted. This was the signal for the artillery to open fire. Along the 8,000 yard front the infantry moved forward.

The mine, which already exploded on 1st July, had now been re-dug and laid. Two companies of the 7th Gordons, forming the extreme right wing of the 51st Division, advanced. They followed the barrage very closely. The Gordons would have been out of sight of the Germans due to the dip in the ground. Along with the barrage and morning fog, this provided some cover, allowing the assault battalions to creep forward on the edge of the barrage, keeping them hidden from German machine guns.[69] Lessons had already been learned from the initial Somme assault. Rather than charge at the German trenches, soldiers went forward at a rate of 25 yards per minute.[70]

66 Bewsher, F.W., The *History of the Fifty First (Highland) Division* (William Blackwood and Sons) 1921, p.11.

67 William Sandison account: Striking Impression of the Ancre Battle, *Shetland News*, 28th December 1916.

68 7th Battalion Gordon Highlanders War Diary. National Archives, WO 95/2882/1.

69 Falls, Cyril, *Life of a Regiment, Vol IV, Official History of the Gordon Highlanders* (Aberdeen University Press) 1958, p.107.

70 Bewsher, F.W., *The History of the Fifty First (Highland) Division* (William Blackwood and Sons) 1921, p.114.

William Sandison stated vividly *'the universe was rent and broken! In successive Company waves we swept into No-man's Land:- and the sight will be blazoned before my eyes until they close for ever.'*[71]

The 51st's machine-gunners on the Bowery, a small tumulus hill near Auchonvillers, laid down a barrage over the attackers' heads.[72] The machine-gun bullets rose upwards then descended, to produce an elliptical 'beaten zone' of bullets, designed to suppress the German long range machine-gun fire and to hinder their advancing reserves. This was a new experience for the men and they were warned that although the bullets would sound as if they were within inches of their heads, they would be travelling many feet above them.[73]

The Gordons came up from the dip into view of the German machine gunners. Hell slipped off its leash. Generally, the Germans were shocked by the intensity of the barrage and how quickly the assault had taken place. The defenders struggled to offer resistance as the Highlanders emerged from the fog. When they reached the German wire, they found it well cut.[74]

Intense fighting continued as daylight came, with the trenches south of Y-Ravine taken. The Gordon Highlanders took line after line of German trenches and reached their first objective, the road linking Beaumont-Hamel to Beaucourt railway station at 6.45 a.m. exactly on time. The 51st divisional boundary was north of the railway station which was in the 63rd [Royal Naval Division] sector. Shetlanders were engaged in this sector also, including Able Seaman Samuel Harper, wounded serving with the Drake Battalion, parents James and Mary originating from Baliasta, Unst. Another wounded RND man was Lieutenant Laurence Mann, of Scarpigarth, Cunningsburgh,

71 William Sandison account: Striking Impression of the Ancre Battle, Shetland News, 28th December 1916.

72 Bewsher, F.W., *The History of the Fifty First (Highland) Division* (William Blackwood and Sons) 1921, p.114.

73 Campbell, C., *Engine of Destruction* (Argyll Publishing) 2013, p.96.

74 Sandison, Dr R., *A Family At War 1914-1918* (Shetland Life) November 1996.

son of Andrew and Janet.[75] The Hood and Drake Battalions captured the railway station at Beaucourt.

Running from east to west a quarter of a mile south of the village of Beaumont-Hamel lay the Y-Ravine - a natural gully 800 yards and 30 feet deep. It was defended by up to four hundred German soldiers, with solid pillboxes and machine guns. The 5th Gordons were drawn in to support and engaged in close combat in and around the Ravine. Y-Ravine itself proved to be the most formidable obstacle for the Division, delaying the advance.[76] Men of the 6th Black Watch and 7th Gordons approached it, and were met with a storm of fire from concealed machine guns and rifles that held them up for several hours. Some of 6th Black Watch skirted the northern side of Y -Ravine and moved on.[77] At one stage more than a hundred men were held down in Y-Ravine by German fire from every quarter. Nearly five hours of fighting took place before resistance began to break. By then the 6th Black Watch and 4th Gordons were moving into the outskirts of Beaumont-Hamel. Progress on the northern end of the village was going well.

William Sandison further described the experience:-

The barrage was on the enemy front line. A filmy mist hung on the ground and in the greying of the dawn the bursting of the shells transmuted its grey whiteness into swirling yellow while the red Artillery flares curved skyward mingling their blood-red with the rolling gambage of the mist. The noise was beyond human belief: through the dull rumbling and dreadful crashing of bursting explosive and shrapnel the overhead fire from Lewis and Vickers guns whistled and screeched their terrible discord. And as we knelt, halfway across, waiting for the barrage to lift, ever before our sight that wondrous red and yellow haze drifted and changed like a great Kaleidoscope. My Platoon officer yelled

---

75 Laurence was later Master Mariner on the s.s. *Florian*. His ship was lost at sea, presumed torpedoed, in the North Atlantic, 20th January, 1941, aged 56. Laurence R. Mann Service File: BT/377/7 National Archives

76 Cave, Nigel, *Somme: Beaumont-Hamel, Newfoundland Park* (Pen and Sword Books) 1997, p.81.

77 Campbell, C., *Engine of Destruction* (Argyll Publishing) 2013. p.102.

7th Gordons Clearing "Y"-Ravine. The 51st Division War Sketches,
by Fred A. Farrell, 1920.   Painting courtesy: Glasgow Museums

*hoarsely - in lieu of whispering, "A Hell's-Fire strafe Corporal:- a
Hell's-fire strafe!"*

*The barrage lifted from the first line and transferred chaos to
the second. Confused by the uproar, choked by the acrid fumes of
high explosive, we stumbled forward, and rushed with bayonet
and bomb on the stupefied Boche! It was over in a minute. Behind
us was the first line: in front of the Ravine. In little bunches with
ranks gapped and broken, we swept on, leaving the wounded
groping helplessly, and dead hideously huddled all about, to
where the black Ravine gaped. Shells and bullets whistled,
shrapnel whine and wailed, men fell fast, and cursed bitterly or
moaned as they fell. The Ravine was stormed and crossed, and in
its sombre depths bombers cleared out the dug-outs and collected
prisoners. No waves now:- nothing of organisation. We staggered
breathlessly forward, wave mixed with wave. The second line is
memory of bayonet plunge and exploding grenade, and on the
heel of that hellish barrage the third line was assaulted.*

On now jumping into the trench I became aware of a numbness in my hand and arm, and on rolling up my sleeve discovered that a bullet had passed through the flesh. What everyone had prayed for: what in anticipation had buoyed up many of those now twisted stiff figures in the Great Adventure, had befallen me:- "a cushy blighty". Reaction now set in, and feeling done and worn, I sat down with a cigarette and looked on, while the remnant of my company consolidated the line and posted sentries.

William's injury was recorded in the *Shetland News* on 23rd November 1916. It was also noted that William's twin brother Thomas had also been wounded in action in France, and that *'both brothers are in hospital in England.'*[78]

The difficult ground made it challenging for the infantry to keep up with the protective artillery barrage. By 07.50 Highlanders were on the German third line, with pockets of enemy holding out. The 4th Gordons were committed from divisional reserve to tackle Y Ravine, bombing from either end. Soldiers of 7th Gordons and 6th Black Watch who had earlier been surrounded in the centre of Y Ravine by Germans who had emerged from their deep dug-outs, stood their ground until they were rescued by Gordon battalion bombers, and elements of their own battalions.[79]

The German second line was breached. Two bombing squads from the 6th Gordons went forward and cleared the third line. This allowed progress to the Green Line, just beyond the Station Road. Fighting became intense and it was impossible to reach the Yellow Line objective at Frankfort Trench.

William added further detail of his experience:-

In yesterday's paper (Daily Mail) Beach Thomas told us all about the Naval Division, and today he has the Scottish Division, so if you read his account you will know all about the old 51st (Highland) 'Crush', of which we form part. You will also see how 'Y' ravine

---

78 William Sandison account: Striking Impression of the Ancre Battle, *Shetland News*, 28th December 1916.

79 Campbell, C., *Engine of Destruction* (Argyll Publishing) 2013, p.102.

was stormed and see how about a platoon of men crept to the base of the 'Y', getting round the flanks and settling down in the 'Sunken Road'. It says they were there at 10 a.m. I have only one correction to make - they were there at 7 a.m. - because I was one of them. We were a mixture of Gordons for the most part, but made up also of Dublin Fusiliers and Marines. We weren't fifty all told and took prisoners out of all proportion to our numbers. It was because we were afraid of being cut off that the Officer sent the Sergt. and me, about 11 o/c, back to find out who held the hill behind us, and it was then that the old sniper, probably a bit hurt at being overlooked, lay in a shell hole on the way back, and potted me through the shoulder. It is a marvel that he didn't 'do me in', because when the sergeant and I were crawling about we spotted him, and he wasn't a hundred yards away. Mind, I don't want you to think I'm bragging, and you needn't tell anybody outside what I'm telling you, but when I'm lying safe here in Hospital I like to think that I was in that small crowd in the Sunken Road.[80]

The 51st waited three more days before relief came through. The objectives of the battle were not achieved. The gains in the marshy lowlands near the river were at great cost. On 19 November, winter rain meant offensive operations were called off.[81]

Source: Manson 1920

Another Shetlander who took part in the Battle of the Ancre was **James Pottinger** from Burra. He joined the 7th Gordon Highlanders in the Armentières Sector in August 1916. With *nothing much to report* initially, he took part in the Ancre advance upon Beaumont-Hamel on 13th November, a *fearful experience. Hundreds of dead, both our men and German, most sickening.*[82] His friend

80 Sandison, Dr R., *A Family At War 1914-1918*, (Shetland Life) November 1996.
81 Cheyne, G.Y., *The Last Great Battle of the Somme, Beaumont-Hamel, 1916* (John Donald) 1988, p.124.
82 Pottinger, James, diary transcript, Shetland Museum and Archives. D1/452.

Pte John William Jamieson, also from Burra, was killed. John was the second son of William and Agnes, Hamnavoe, Burra Isle, aged 19. He had been in France for a short period, the greater part of on the front line. Before the war, he had worked for Taylor & Blance, bakers. It was mentioned that *word had been received in Burra Isle from Private Jamieson's chum stating that he got one of his legs shot away, to which he succumbed.*[83] James Pottinger added how only 22 of his company of 120 came out of the battle unscathed.[84] **John William is buried at the Y-Ravine Cemetery.**

Also killed nearby was **Laurence Halcrow** of the 7th Battalion, of 25 Burgh Road, Lerwick. He was the son of Francis and Williamina. When writing to his mother, the officer conveying the news mentioned *he understood that that he was killed while advancing on the German lines,* adding that Laurence was a *good soldier and his death was greatly regretted by the men in the platoon.* Another Lerwick soldier who took part in the same attack, Private Charles Halcrow of Mounthooly Street, mentioned that Laurence was killed *on the edge of the German parapet.* His mother received two letters from her son only the week before. She said that his news was *bright and cheerful.*[85] Laurence was another A.E.I. pupil. He is buried close to John William Jamieson in Y-Ravine Cemetery.

The 153rd Brigade's assessment concluded that:- *the mist ... helped the attack ... zero hour was too early and the darkness caused loss of direction ... the bombardment over a long period undoubtedly deceived the enemy and he had given up expecting an attack ... the front of our attack was too extended for the number of men available ... and if the element of surprise had been lacking the attack might easily have failed.*[86]

83 *Shetland News*, 30th November, 1916.
84 Pottinger James, diary transcript, Shetland Museum and Archives. D1/452.
85 Shetland News, 30th November 1916.
86 Campbell, C., *Engine of Destruction* (Argyll Publishing) 2013. p.110.

With daylight intense fighting persisted. This experience was detailed again by **William David Arthur**:-

I saw men go down by the light from the bursting shells, but I could not make out who it was. On we went, however, behind our barrage fire with but one intention – to get to Fritz. We reached his front line, but his trench had been laid flat with our shells and there was nobody in it. So on we went, taking his second, third and fourth lines likewise, and encountering very little resistance.[87]

We made a lot of prisoners in the dug-outs of his fourth line, and I must say that they showed up the courage of what the Kaiser calls his "incomparable" army. They came out of the dug outs, trembling like leaves, with their hands up, and howling for mercy. By the time we got the prisoners out it was seven o'clock, and I was sent back with an important message. I had one prisoner with me, and had got only half way back when a sniper got me in the left thigh with a bullet. I dropped in a shell hole, and the German who was along with me bound up my wound. He also gave me cigars and everything he could think of, for he thought I would take revenge on him. However, I sent him off with another batch of prisoners, and I lay in the shell hole till 12 o'clock. Then Fritz's shells began to fall rather close. One dropped just alongside practically burying me. One piece of shrapnel tore the haversack off my back, but I was unhurt. I thought then that it was getting too warm, so I chanced it. The sniper still had his eye on me, so I had to be careful how I moved. I got my rifle as a crutch, and I shoved and crawled from one shell hole to another till I got over the top of the ridge. Then I was safe from that sniper. I managed to get about a hundred yards, but my leg was giving me so much pain owing to the exertion that I had to give in and wait again. In a few minutes I saw another lot of prisoners coming, and I crawled along again till I reached the road they had to come up. I got one of them to give me a hand, and he helped me to our first dressing station. The Doctor had a look at my bandage, and said I was quite all right. After getting a drink of water and lighting

87 With the 'Terriers' on the Ancre, Interesting Narrative of the Big Push', *Shetland News*, 21st December 1916.

a fag, I made my way again for down the line. This time I was helped and half carried by two R.A.M.C. chaps. The shells were bursting all around, but somehow I paid no heed to them but walked on. At last I got down to where we had a light railway, and got one of the trollies which took me down the line. There I got another two Germans to give me a hand to the ambulances, and if you had seen me coming down you would have laughed just as the artillery boys did when I passed the back of the guns which were in action. The two Germans could easily stand under my armpits, and the boys asked if I could not find any larger ones. I told them I just took two to make up. They all got round about these two Germans, and they did not leave a button or anything but what they took as souvenirs.[88]

William Arthur then related his further experiences at the clearing station and base hospital.

Well I eventually got to the dressing station, and from there to the base, and now here I am in a private hospital. The doctor and nurses are all very nice and there are only six men in the ward with me so we have good times, and as there are always plenty of visitors it is quite lightsome. I always weary a good bit because I haven't been used to this confinement, but I can't do anything else and we have learned to put with the things after being across in France.[89]

I can't tell you how much I enjoyed the nice clean bed at the hospital after the muddy trenches, and the trenches are in some mess now – up to the waist in mud and slush. I assure you that it was terrible, and it is no wonder that I am contented to lie here in peace away from it all. I consider myself lucky when I think of how my chums have fared.[90]

Notification of William's injury was published in the *Shetland News*. It was noted that he had written a letter on 7th November

---

88 *Shetland News*, 21st December, 1916.
89 *Shetland News*, 14th December, 1916.
90 *Shetland News*, 14th December, 1916.

when out of the trenches, but he had expected to be sent forward within days.[91]

He continued:- *I would like to tell you all about it, but it would take too long, so I will just give you it in brief. You will have seen in the papers about our last advance on the Ancre front. Well we made the charge at dawn on the morning of the 13th and swept the Germans right out of their fourth line, and took the ridge and village of* [Beaumont-Hamel].[92]

After referring to the terrible experience which he passed through, **William Arthur** asked his sister to forward him the local papers. He was very anxious to know how the Shetland boys fared. He concluded by saying that he lost everything but his cigarette case. As the battalion did not pay when a man was in hospital he would just have to borrow. *'There's no other way out of it, but I will get along somehow.'*[93]

By the early afternoon, elements of the 51st moved into the outskirts of the Beaumont-Hamel village. The 4th Gordons were involved by this stage, meeting up with their 'sister' battalion, the 7th. Given the number of Shetlanders involved in both, it is almost certain that meetings took place amongst men from home. The afternoon was spent clearing the ruins and cellars of the village.

A German soldier, Fahnrich Pukall's take on the Battle further resonates:-

Then came the shout that Schrott was dead .... He had been hit in the temple by a bullet. He lay there in front of me in the floor of the trench. He had been a friend to all; tirelessly he worked for the common good. His experience had been indispensable, as had his presence in battle. Now he was not more. I did not want to believe it. But there was not time for mourning. I had to decide what to do. Our flanks were up in the air; there were British soldiers all around us. To our right, hordes of them were advancing down the road from Auchonvillers to Beaumont.[94]

91 *Shetland News*, 30th November, 1916.
92 *Shetland News*, 14th December, 1916.
93 *Shetland News*, 14th December, 1916.
94 Shelden, Jack, *The German Army On The Somme, 1914-1916* (Pen & Sword) 2012. p.374-5.

The enemy on the 51st's front was the 12th Division. A German enquiry correctly attributed the defeat in part to the false sense of security generated by the numerous days of bombardment without attacks; the mist, making accurate German artillery fire difficult; the quality of the 12th Division, deemed to be unreliable, allowing itself to be surprised. The divisional commander had not taken a grip on the battle and German First Army headquarters had taken control of it. The accusation that the defenders were taken by surprise has to be balanced against the closeness that elements of the 51st followed the barrage into the German trenches.[95] It was added that German troops of the 12th Division defending this position, were too slow to reach the fire-steps from the dugouts, and men were taken by surprise, and had to engage right away in hand-to hand combat in which the numerical superiority of the British worked to their advantage[96]

Photograph courtesy:
Martin Emslie

James Houston recorded in his diary this day:-

Got up at 5 a.m. Breakfast at 6 a.m. Told to stand by ready to move away at any time. The guns started to roar at a quarter to six & what a noise they did make. 8 a.m. our Division had taken the German's third line and a lot of prisoners. Marched up to the trenches. Left Billet at 9 a.m. We went over the top at 3 p.m. We saw no Germans and marched up to fill a gap between two other Regiments. Got there at night & we were told afterwards that 400 Germans ran away when they saw us coming. We were very lucky for had the Germans made a stand on the ridge with a machine gun they could have wiped us all out. We started to dig a trench in the ridge. But we were not long started

95 Campbell, C., *Engine of Destruction* (Argyll Publishing) 2013, p.110.
96 Duffy, Christopher, *Through German Eyes: The British and The Somme*, 1916 (Phoenix) 2006, p.258.

Battle of the Ancre: counting the prisoners as they came in from Beaumont-Hamel, captured by the 51st (Highland) Division, 13 November 1916.
Photo courtesy: Imperial War Museum

before we were shelled by our own guns. Some fellows were wounded. We were not long in flying back again. We had gone too far forward & the artillery thought we were Germans. We went back later on & began to dig again. Dug all night.[97]

Writing further to his wife, James added:- *I was in the advance on the 13th of November. We went over the top in the afternoon and were told that we were to fill the gap between two regiments. Well, we got up and went right over the German third line. The only Germans we saw were prisoners coming in and those lying dead and wounded. The prisoners were quite happy to be taken, and they have some of the boys' cigarettes and cigars. A fellow in our Company who was on trench control says that after the boys had gone over the top he saw some Germans some distance away in shell holes looking towards him. He waved his arms as much as to say "Come on", and about 40 came running to him - glad to be taken prisoners.*

The Battalion War Diary notes that there was intense fighting clearing the German trenches.[98]

James added:- *We came to some German dugouts, and they were deep down, with two entrances, and each had a small stove, also beds, or rather bunks, one above the other, with spring bottoms, so they evidently intended to be comfortable. We came across plenty of food, also tea and sugar, and some of the boys found barrels of beer and rum, and bottles of champagne. We were up at that place for four days, and the time passed fine. There was plenty of excitement exploring the dug outs. We were all sitting in a shell hole one day when a shell burst unexpectedly, killing and wounding about 20 men, but I did not get a scratch. You can imagine that there was some excitement at the time. We only got relieved in the trenches on Sunday, and we had to march a good distance afterwards. It was therefore late at night before we reached camp. We were all wet and covered with mud, so on Monday we were all very busy getting our clothes dried and cleaned.*[99]

97 Diary of Private James Houston, Gordon Highlanders, courtesy of Martin Emslie.
98 4th Battalion Gordon Highlanders, War Diary, WO 95/2880/4, National Archives.
99 *Shetland News*, 14th December, 1916

A field ambulance soldier noted upon entering a German dugout he descended about forty steps to a large floored and timbered chamber about fifty feet long. At one end, a second set of steps led to a similar chamber. One side was lined with a double layer of bunks that was filled with dead and wounded Germans. Most of these men had been casualties in the early morning of the 13th. There was mention of rats squeaking and scuttling away from feeding on dead bodies on the floor when lights were flashed.[100]

William Sandison's father Andrew wrote about William and Tom's wounds to their other sibling Christopher, 24th November 1916:-

On Sunday (19th. November), a telegram came from Daisy that the boys were both wounded and in hospital in England ... that their wounds were not severe...Willie at Norwich and Tom at Shrewsbury. They had been at the big fight on the Ancre on the 13th. We have had an anxious wait; owing to the N. of S. Coys. new arrangements and the vagaries of the weather the mails have been very irregular of late. But we got letters this morning - a card from Willie and a few lines from Tom, both dated 17th:- a whole week getting letters from England!. W. does not say of his wound:- just that he is in hospital; but the card is signed and addressed by himself. Tom, shot through the left shoulder, I will give you the most of his epistle:- 'Do not be alarmed when I tell you I am in Hospital and in Blighty. A sniper got me in the left shoulder on the morning of the 13th. We advanced at 6 a.m. and at 7 were in the German fourth line. At 8.30 we were hauling prisoners by the score and smoking cigars, and at 11.30 as I was going back a message a sniper whom we had passed over got me. The bullet went in my back and came out the top of my shoulder. I had a stiff job getting back because old Fritz still had his eye on me, but by this time I have got as far back as Ward XIII Berrington Hospital, near Shrewsbury. Don't be anxious. I am being treated well, food, bed, Sisters, Nurses are great. It was a great fight.

---

100 Campbell, C., *Engine of Destruction* (Argyll Publishing) 2013, p.110

We'd been expecting it these last few weeks, but the Allyman was taken absolutely by surprise.[101]

On 14th December 1916 Andrew wrote again to Christopher:-

On the 22nd. November I wrote you a brief note that the boys were both hit in the big fight on the Ancre on the 13th November. Willie got a bullet through the right forearm - a clean wound, with no bones broken, and he is now almost well, being at the convalescent hospital. Tom's wound was more severe - a sniper got him in the back; the bullet entering between the shoulders and coming put at the top of the left shoulder, making an ugly exit wound. He is getting round all right, but it will take much more time than Willie's. I have been copying out, in duplicate, some of their 'yarns' for you and Andrew, [brother of William and Tom] *thinking you would find it interesting. We have had a very anxious time but we are thankful for them to be in England for a little time, and hoping to see them home. One is in Norfolk County and the other in Shropshire, the width of England between, and have not seen each other since the day before the battle. This last fight has been a sad one for Shetland, as nearly 30 of the boys have been killed and wounded. The 'Gordons' as usual were in the thick of it. It has been an anxious time but we are keeping well.*
Love from all -Your loving father.[102]

Following the war, both Tom and William had interesting lives. William remained in the army until 1921, serving in Kurdistan and Mesopotamia. Returning to Britain, he went to Edinburgh University, afterwards marrying Roberta Frances Fraser, daughter of Robert Fraser, a Scalloway merchant. He lived for 20 years in Shropshire, and retired in Aberdeen, dying 20th April, 1979. He wrote two books. "A Shetland Merchant's Day Book in 1762", was published in 1934, and competently illustrated by William. It was dedicated to his father Andrew. The second, "Shetland Verse:- Remnants of the Norn", was published in 1953. William

101 Sandison, Dr R., *A Family At War 1914-1918* (Shetland Life) November 1996.
102 Sandison, Dr R., *A Family At War 1914-1918* (Shetland Life) November 1996.

was a supporter of the Communist Party in the years following World War One, and contributed some poems to 'The Worker'. He followed this up with support for the Labour movement.

One of his best poems was written as a memorial following the death of J.J. Haldane Burgess.[103]

After the Second World War, William started writing for the newly launched "New Shetlander" and the Shetland Archive holds a series of letters from him to the editor, Peter Jamieson, written between 1950 and 1967. After an absence of 19 years, he visited Shetland in 1953. In all those years he makes only one reference to his service in the First World War, but it is a poignant one:-

He wrote on 13th November 1967:- *'It's fifty-one years today since I was wounded. Hit's no muckle winder as a'm feelin kinda aald. On 13th. November, 1916, fifty years and eternity seemed synonymous.'*[104]

Twin brother Tom also went to Edinburgh University and qualified with an M.A. in 1922. He trained as a teacher at Moray House College of Education and taught in various schools, eventually becoming headmaster of Strathdon school 1938 - 1945. After the war he temporarily left teaching for surveying work, then returned to the profession to become a part-time lecturer in mathematics at the Technical College in Llanelly, Carmarthenshire. He passed away in 1977.[105]

Two boys at the Ancre, who achieved so much in life. William wrote from hospital, referring to his own personal loss:-

I had a letter from Tom ... Bill Robertson [killed] who was at the Institute [The Anderson Educational Institute, now the Anderson High School] with us. And I can get no word of the Clunesses. Altogether it seems a ghastly affair [106]

---

103 J.J. Haldane Burgess was an important supporter of the Marxist Social and Democratic Federation created in Lerwick in 1905. He is probably best remembered for the Up Helly Aa' song, sung to this day at every burning of the galley. William's memorial poem was entitled "Yule Song". It appeared in the *Shetland News* on 27th January 1927.

104 Peter Jamieson Collection, Shetland Museum and Archives. D9/275.

105 Sandison, Dr R., *A Family At War 1914-1918* (Shetland Life) November 1996.

106 Sandison, Dr R., *A Family At War 1914-1918* (Shetland Life) November 1996.

Thiepval Memorial, Picardy, France.   Photo: Jon Sandison

OTHERS WHO WERE LEFT

Those that did not come home could not tell their story. Often they have their names engraved on the Thiepval Memorial. On its wall panels are the names of those of the British and South African forces who were killed, of whom no remains were found, during all the battles of the Somme, 72,191 in all. There are 29 Shetland-linked names on it.[107] Eight of these were killed during the Ancre. The Memorial is the largest British battle memorial in the world, and was inaugurated by the Prince of Wales, later King Edward VIII, on 1st August 1932. The following men have their name on the Memorial.

Tragically, James Sinclair was the only son of Robert and Barbara, 26 Albany Street, Lerwick. The officer conveying news of **Private James W Sinclair's** death told his mother he

---

107 Database on Shetland Service and Loss in the Army, First World War. Jon Sandison.

was unable to give precise details, but assured people that he had *fought and died gallantly.* Aged 19 he had worked in the County Clerk's Office, leaving for service in the summer of 1915. In July of 1916, he got embarkation leave and paid a short visit to his parents in Lerwick. Robert had *considerable musical attainments,* and for a time was a drummer in the Lerwick Brass Band. Recently he had applied for a commission as a Lieutenant, *which he would undoubtedly have got if he had come through the great Ancre battle ... a smart and intelligent young man and had a career of much promise before him. His tall erect figure gave him a fine soldierly bearing, and we have little doubt the spirit which induced him to offer his youthful services to his country in the dark months of the autumn of 1914 was ever with him right up to the end.*[108]

Territorial **Private William Kay** was the son of Shetlanders William and Williamina, staying in Liverpool. His mother died nine days after his birth from puerperal fever, and William was sent back to Lerwick to be brought up by his grandparents.[109] William was a grandson of the then late David Kay of 47 Burgh Road. He had been employed as a cooper with A. Wood & Sons. William was in the first draft of the Territorials which was dispatched to France. He was widely known among younger members of the community, and *held in highest esteem* by his many friends. He was particularly popular among local footballers and was one of the leading members of the local Thistle team. The report mentioned that *sturdily built and active in movement, he was one of the best full backs in the town, and played in the last inter-county match ... those who knew and admired him are assured that "Chum"* as he was known to them *– met his end with that rare spirit which ever characterised him.*[110]

108 *Shetland News*, 30th November, 1916.
109 Shetland Family History Society.
110 *Shetland News*, 30th November, 1916

One other casualty with a local connection was **David Harold Evans**. Known as Harold, he was born in Glamorganshire, the son of David and Adelina Sarah, of Custom House, Blacktoft, Howden, Yorkshire. Upon the outbreak of war, he was part of the Sandwick cable guard. There was a note about Harold in the *Shetland Times* in April 1917. It mentioned that *there were few better known young men in Lerwick, and certainly none more popular.* Harold had arrived at Lerwick as an Official in H.M. Customs and Excise. He had enlisted in the local Territorials upon war being declared, age 26 ... *of a bright and cheerful disposition, the deceased made many friends, and his musical attainments made him a favourite with everyone.*[111] As he was not local, David's picture was not in the Roll of Honour, but it was in the local press.

The *Shetland News* mentions a letter *from one of the Shetland soldiers ... that Pte. W. Kay and Pte. D.H. Evans were buried together. Some of the Shetland lads were present at the burial.*[112] Sadly it can only be assumed that their bodies were lost subsequently on the battlefield, hence their commemoration on Thiepval.

Every loss had its own family story, but a family story so closely linked to the Front was borne out by the loss of **Private George Groat**. George was aged 20, the youngest son of John and Ann, his father a baker in Lerwick. Like many others, George had joined the Territorials when the war broke out. This was described *as might have been expected of a member of this patriotic family, at once responded when the call was made for volunteers for Imperial Service.* He was in the first lot of Shetland Gordons to have crossed to France, and as a result had been about 12 months at the Front. George was *a very likeable young man, and had a wide circle of friends among younger members of the community.* He was one of the original team

111 *Shetland Times*, 17th April, 1917
112 *Shetland News*, 30th November, 1916.

members of the Rangers Football Team, a *keen and enthusiastic player*. In a real "Band of Brothers" context, the newspaper mentions further how three other brothers were at that point in France. They were Alexander, David and John. Both Alexander and David were also in the 7th Gordons. Alexander was also wounded at the Ancre. He had an operation to remove a bullet. Not long before George was killed, the four brothers in France had met at the Front after having been *separated for quite a long time*.[113] Now one was be separated for ever.

Source: Manson 1920

Another of the Territorials lost was Lance Corporal **Magnus Christie** from Cunningsburgh, son of Laurence and Robina. The *Shetland News* said that Mrs Christie, Skibhoul, Cunningsburgh, had received a letter from 2nd Lieut. Henderson, Gordons that *her son Lance–Corporal Christie was killed on the night of 18th November during the heavy fighting in France. A piece of shell hit him, and though he was attended to at once, he died about an hour after*. It was then mentioned that Magnus had *only been a few days with us, but had proved himself a most capable non-commissioned officer, and a cheery comrade in the trenches*. The message went on:- *accept my deepest sympathy, and the sympathy of all the company in your great loss. I regret that I have been unable to write to you before, but the battalion had only just returned to the trenches*. The newspaper said that *Magnus was only 19 years of age ... a very bright, capable lad*. Before the war he was in the grocery trade, and was a *general favourite*. His last employment had been with Mr G. Hall, Lerwick. He had joined the Territorials when war broke out and had been with the Gordons ever since. He had been at the base in France helping to train men, and had only been

---

113 *Shetland News*, 30th November, 1916

something like ten days in the trenches before he was killed. Upon the outbreak of war, Magnus was a member of the Sandwick cable guard.

Others were found, and buried. Another loss at the Ancre was **Private George Spence**, the eldest son of James and Helen, Nornagarth, Cullivoe, and assistant teacher at Greenbank Public School when war broke out. He was born in Edinburgh before his parents moved back to Yell.[114] He was reported as wounded and missing. George had been stationed at Greenock, had further training in England, then crossed over to France in June 1916. He had taken part in the initial assault on the Somme during the summer. George was the first boy to achieve a Secondary Education Bursary at Cullivoe Public School for several years. He was two years at the Institute in Lerwick before being assistant teacher at Greenbank. His intention was to finish his college course as a teacher, but *he gave all up to serve his king and country*. In perhaps typical Shetland fashion, the report stated that George was an *unassuming quiet lad and was much respected by all who knew him*. He was only 21.[115] George is buried at the Ancre Cemetery, Beaumont-Hamel.

Private Andrew Simpson, aged 22, was formerly in the employment of John Henry, butcher, but afterwards served his apprenticeship as a cooper. He was the second youngest son of Andrew and Philadelphia of St Magnus Street, and was working at this trade when war broke out. Andrew went over to France with the first draft, and had seen a good deal of service. Private Simpson was known as a *bright and intelligent lad, and a clever workman*. His brothers James and John were also in

---

114 Shetland Family History Society.
115 *Shetland News*, 23rd March, 1917.

the local Territorials.[116] James had been recently home on leave after recovering from shell shock.[117] Andrew is also buried in the Ancre Cemetery at Beaumont-Hamel.

Also killed was **Robert Coutts** from Pilot Lane, Lerwick, son of James and Wilhelmina, aged 21, a clerk in the North of Scotland and Town and County Bank. He too had left with the original draft. When at the Lerwick Central School, Robert had shown *considerable ability, and was one of the most promising pupils at the school. He was a very capable and trustworthy clerk.*[118] Robert is buried at the Varennes Military Cemetery. His brother John was also wounded at the Ancre, then killed just over a year later at the Battle of Cambrai. John had been employed as a baker with Malcolmson & Co.[119]

Lance-Corporal Alexander Cluness, son of John and Mary Cluness, Rockfield, Unst, fought at the Ancre in November 1916. Later wounded at the Battle of Arras in 1917, he returned to the front and was finally demobilised after the Armistice. He finished the war a Sergeant in a Gordons pioneer battalion, clearing ammunition dumps. For rescuing a fellow Shetlander from No Man's Land under heavy fire at the Somme, Alec won the Military Medal for bravery. The *Shetland News* commended him on the award *He is to be heartily congratulated on having performed a deed which has entitled him to the Military Medal.*[120]

Alec wrote to his friend Robert Coutts's mother in February 1917:- *I saw the death of your son Robbie announced in the Shetland Times ... During the time he was with us, Robbie proved himself one of the best of soldiers:- always ready to do his share of work, and always cheerful, even under trying circumstances. Indeed, he was one of the pluckiest soldiers in*

116 Shetland Family History Society.
117 *Shetland News*, 30th November,1916.
118 *Shetland News*, 23rd November, 1916.
119 *Shetland News*, 30th November, 1916.
120 *Shetland News*, 1st March, 1917.

the whole regiment ... I can only assure you of my sympathy, and may it be a consolation to know that he fell doing his duty to the last.

Soon after the war, Alec and his brother Andrew returned to the Somme battlefields on a motorcycle, revisiting the places where the Shetlanders fought and died.

Alec died on 24 February 1964.[121]

Source: Manson 1920

Gilbert Smith, died of wounds on 26th November 1916 aged 33. Son of John and Lily Smith of Uyeasound, Unst, his father was a farm grieve. Gilbert is buried at Wimereux Communal Cemetery 5 kilometres north of Boulogne. Very close to him is the grave of Lieutenant-Colonel John McCrae, the Canadian doctor and author of the famous poem *In Flanders Fields*. Gilbert was employed as a cooper in Lerwick before joining the local Territorials. He was seriously wounded on 13th November, and had to have his left leg amputated. His condition deteriorated, and he died on 23rd November. John and Lily had 13 children. Two of Gilbert's brothers were also killed in the war; Andrew, also a Gordon Highlander, died October 1916, while Francis, a Cameron Highlander, died in June 1918. A heartbreaking loss for any community, not least the close one of Uyeasound.

---

121 Alex Cluness notes.

SAFELY WOUNDED

The initial list in the *Shetland Times*, under the heading *Heavy Casualty List. Shetland Lads Supreme Sacrifice*, had 20 men wounded, with brothers Thomas and William Sandison, as well as William D Arthur on that list.[122] The list of the wounded was extensive and grew further as the days and weeks wore on. Some wounded later perished. Among the wounded and recorded as being in hospital was William Oakes. He was the son of Edwin and Margaret, Church Lane, Lerwick. In 1917 William was killed in the Ypres sector. Also wounded was William Smith, son of James and Joan Smith, Hillside Cottage, Upper Sound, Lerwick. He had been wounded in the head by shell fragments during the battle near Serre He later died of gunshot wounds in January 1918.

Others came home, to live out their lives.

The following letter was received by John Simpson, a Sandness school teacher from his son James:-

I was admitted to hospital on 13th November and discharged on the 20th. I'm all right now, I only had slight wounds in the head. I wish it had been a little worse, and I might have got "blighty". I was hit in the forehead with shrapnel. One bit hit my eye. I've three or four cuts in the brow. My shrapnel helmet saved me as it splintered on the helmet, and only the wee bits got me. I'll soon be going back to the battalion. I hope I'm sent to the 7th Gordons again.[123]

Another, John W Nicolson, of Union Street, Lerwick wrote a letter to his mother following being wounded:-

I am presently in hospital with a shrapnel wound in the back of the neck received in the Battle of the Ancre. You will no doubt

---

122 *Shetland Times*, 2nd December, 1916.
123 *Shetland News*, 7th December, 1916.

have read all about it in the papers. We went over the top on Monday morning at 5:45, thus starting the great attack on the German lines which has won us so many prisoners and before which fell the villages of Beaumont-Hamel, Beaucourt etc. It was a dark misty morning when we started ... I had just reached the parapet of the German front line when I got struck. I didn't know at that time whether it was serious or not, but I crawled into a shell hole, where I lay for a few minutes and then made for the German trench just a few yards in front, where most of our chaps had already arrived. I got the wound dressed by a stretcher bearer, and was in the trench until about four in the afternoon, when I managed to get back to our own lines.

He went on to describe how he had to go under x-rays so that the surgeons could locate and remove pieces of shrapnel. He concluded by saying:- *We had roped in about 4000 prisoners when I left the trenches and I see they are still coming in, so I think we can't grumble seeing that the attack was such a great success.*[124]

124 *Shetland News*, 30th November, 1916.

LEGACY

With dawn on 14th November and post-battle exhaustion, those that had come through this part of the battle waited three more days before its relief came. They had been in the line for six continuous weeks. The 51st was noted to be in high spirits when they finally went down the line on the 17th November.[125]

General Harper, speaking in 1922 said:

When the Division proceeded there the place had been attacked on at least two occasions, and it still remained intact. When I went to those Divisions that had attacked in order to try to get some tips, I was told, 'You have not a dog's chance.' .... Yet Beaumont-Hamel was taken, you might say, with almost automatic precision.[126]

The overall fighting cost the British approximately 420,000 casualties, and the French just over 200,000. German losses have been difficult to quantify, with estimates ranging from 500,00 to over 600,00.[127] By November Haig was desperate for something that could be described as a success; the weather would prevent attack throughout the winter. An advance of just 1,000 or 2,000 yards would be a positive end to the campaign.[128] Allied leaders met in November at Chantilly, and agreed that it was time to stop for the winter.

It could be said that for all of the success announced from Beaumont-Hamel, 116 days after it had been scheduled to fall, the results were modest. When the battle ended in mid-November the British had pushed the Germans back to Bapaume, which was to have been taken in the first week.[129] The maximum advance

125 Cheyne, G.Y., *The Last Great Battle of the Somme, Beaumont-Hamel, 1916* (John Donald) 1988, p.134.
126 Rorie, D., *A Medico's Luck in the War,* (Naval and Military Press), 1929, p.104-105.
127 Sheffield, G., *The Somme* (Cassell Military Paperbacks) 2003, p.151.
128 Prior, Robin and Wilson, Trevor, *The Somme* (Yale University Press) 2005, p.294.
129 Holmes, Richard, *Tommy. The British Soldier On The Western Front* (Harper Collins Publishers), 2004. p.47.

was just over 2,000 yards, and the amount of territory gained was not significant. Equally the infantry of two divisions at the Ancre, had been utilised for no great purpose.[130]

Historical opinions have been split on the Somme, with debate continuing unabated. Some view it as the 'nadir' of the British Army.[131] It seemed at the time that the country would never get over the Somme, and it never has.[132]

At every phase of the Somme, including the Ancre, the British army adopted new tactics and incorporated progressive technology. At Beaumont-Hamel the 51st's leapfrog system of attack had been proved, and experience gained from which the future training of the Division evolved.[133] The volunteer army learned many lessons in command transforming into an experienced force.[134]. The battle was a watershed in the history of the British army in the war.[135] But it was clear to all that the burden of 1916 had, for the British and French alike, been unsupportable. On the German side, Ludendorff acknowledged that his army was exhausted by this stage.[136] The Germans had learned many lessons too. Both armies had brutal learning curves in a finely balanced war, sides with different strengths, but quite equally matched for much of the conflict. Some historians argue that the "war winning" army of 1918 began its life on the Somme in 1916.[137] A long 25 months later, on ground a few miles from the objectives of 1st July, the British army would advance 8 miles in one day, an unheard of gain in 1916. Whatever way this debate sways, it matters not. Our boys were engaged in it, and contributed significantly throughout.

130 Prior, Robin and Wilson, Trevor, *The Somme* (Yale University Press) 2005, p.299.
131 Prior, Robin and Wilson, Trevor, *The Somme* (Yale University Press) 2005, p.315.
132 Macdonald, Lyn, *Somme* (Penguin Books, 1983), p.xiii
133 Bewsher, F.W., *The History of the Fifty First (Highland) Division* (William Blackwood and Sons) 1921, p.120.
134 Holmes, Richard, *The Western Front* (Ebury Publishing) 1999, p.153.
135 Holmes, Richard, *Tommy. The British Soldier On The Western Front* (Harper Collins Publishers), 2004. p.48.
136 Holmes, Richard, *The Western Front* (Ebury Publishing) 1999, p.152.
137 Sheffield, G., *The Somme,* (Cassell Military Paperbacks) 2003, p.163.

Perhaps the ultimate marker for the Somme is that the Kaiser's troops had to withdraw to more easily defensible positions. Whilst academic debate measures the loss of boys from communities such as Shetland, we can remember the three individual local lads who lie nearby to each other in Queen's Cemetery, or have their names inscribed on the same Gordon Highlanders' panel at Thiepval.

Ancre panel, Thiepval memorial.   Photo: Jon Sandison

The overall casualties for 51st for the Ancre phase included 30 officers killed in action, 78 wounded, 3 missing. For the rank and file, 494 were killed in action with 1381 wounded, 194 missing, a total of 2,180. Bewsher's total was 123 officers and 2355 other ranks killed, wounded or missing.[138] The 2nd Division, on the

138 Bewsher, F.W., *The History of the Fifty First (Highland) Division* (William Blackwood and Sons) 1921, p.123

51st's immediate left, lost nearly 3,000 men, and gained little ground, and the 3rd, to its left, lost 2,400, for no gain.[139] Here, like many other communities in the Highlands and Islands of Scotland, Shetland's loss resonated.

The loss of 22 Shetland men, one hundred years on, still cannot be forgotten; eight of them former pupils of the Anderson Educational Institute. Sadness and sense of loss was felt throughout the Shetland in Christmas 1916. Family life, Christmas, and home would never be the same again for so many.

139 Campbell, C., *Engine of Destruction* (Argyll Publishing) 2013, p.110

LOCAL IMPACT

Within weeks the local press reported that *Not until last weekend has the County, but especially Lerwick, received the news of the loss of so many young lives in one action.* It added that *when it became known that the Shetland Territorials had taken part in the battle of the Ancre, details of casualties were awaited with deep anxiety, and the fear that our local soldiers might have suffered heavily proved eventually to be true ... It was known, of course, that the Shetland Gordons were on the Ancre, and that they would be in the big offensive, and people, not only those who had sons or brothers in France, but also those who had not, would be prepared for casualties.*[140]

Prior to the Ancre, there had been much loss to Shetland. But the cost of this war to the community had now become unfathomable. The impact home was described by the *Shetland News* at the end of November. It was a sober, yet understandable – and to others – upon reflection, perhaps a stark image.

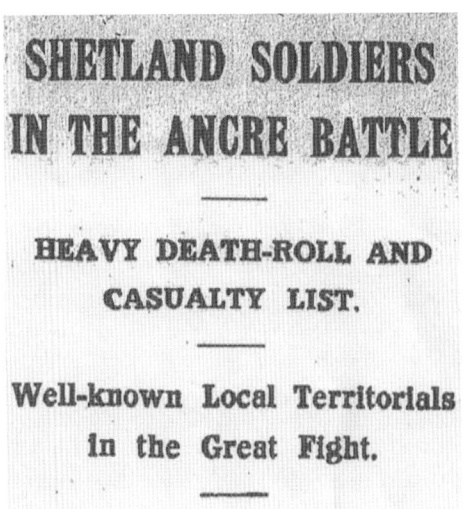

SHETLAND SOLDIERS IN THE ANCRE BATTLE

HEAVY DEATH-ROLL AND CASUALTY LIST.

Well-known Local Territorials in the Great Fight.

Headline from *The Shetland News*, 30th November, 1916.

---

140 *Shetland News*, 30th November, 1916.

We are but a small community, and the killed are so well known to everyone that it comes in the form of a personal loss. And, to many homes it means that all they had in the form of earthly happiness has been laid on the altar of patriotism. To them the keystone had dropped out of life.[141]

The News went on to state that news of casualties obtained by parents of soldiers concerned *conveyed the first sad intelligence, but later in the day is was learned that Provost Goodlad had received a letter from 2nd Lieut D. Peterson containing a list of eleven killed, eleven wounded and two missing. There were signs everywhere of the shock the town had got, while many homes were plunged into mourning by the sad news which it was the Provost's painful duty to break. ....*[142]

The impact of this excruciating wait for so many was further described by how the intervening period was an anxious time for many. When news eventually did come, the effect that this had on the community as a whole was also clearly detailed.

Along Commercial Street little groups of men, women and young people could be seen talking, some anxiously, some expectantly, yet all seriously and sympathetically. All were out to glean further news and gather fresh details:- the public anxiety was symbolic of the very deep personal interest which everyone in Lerwick takes in the Shetland Territorials.

By Saturday and Sunday, many of the wounded in Lieut. Peterson's list were identified. Each new post brought the news of more deaths. People waited between the Friday and Tuesday for another post. News from the front was displayed next to the Post Office outside the news room, with telegrams being posted up on the board.

Parents lost sons, girls lost boyfriends, sons and daughters lost brothers, and many lost friends. Rather ominously, it was *feared* that there *may still be further casualties, but until definite news*

---

141 *Shetland News*, 30th November, 1916.
142 *Shetland News*, 30th November, 1916.

comes it is impossible to estimate the toll which the great fight on the Ancre has exacted from the ranks of the Shetlands Gordons. Tragically, the report mentioned how the death roll contained the names of four only sons, *a very high percentage of the total. The death of an only son, leaves an everlasting blank and an irreplaceable loss.*[143]

The *Shetland Times* noted that in *all Lerwick Churches on Sunday last, special references were made to the sad calamity which had overtaken the community, by the falling in action in France of so many of our young men. In each case the references were couched in most appropriate language, and many of the hearers were visibly affected.*[144]

The harsh reality that so many would not now be coming home gripped our community. Their home would remain in France, encapsulated in this moment of time. There are three cemeteries in the Newfoundland Memorial Park alone:- The Y-Ravine Cemetery, Hunter's Cemetery, and Hawthorn Ridge Cemetery. Hunter's Cemetery is located near to the 51st Highland Division Memorial, and is a very unusual cemetery design. Forty-six soldiers of the 51st who fell during the taking of Beaumont-Hamel were buried here in a large shellhole. The headstones do not mark individual graves, but are set into a central wall around the Cross of Sacrifice. Those Shetlanders wounded at the Ancre were taken to clearing stations. Those who died afterward are buried elsewhere. Those who were killed outright, if they were fortunate to have a marked grave, were buried in and around the battlefield.

During World War One, the Anderson Educational Institute lost 49 former pupils alone. Seven of those Territorials killed during the Battle of the Ancre were former pupils. Two years later with the Armistice of 1918, Rector Joseph Kirton reflected on this loss. Former pupil John Johnston spoke about this moment in the school's 100th Anniversary Centenary magazine. He mentions how Mr Kirton was taking a History class:-

---

143   *Shetland News*, 30th November, 1916.
144   *Shetland Times*, 2nd December, 1916.

Suddenly at 11 a.m. on that memorable day, there bust out a wild pealing of bells from the Town Hall, and an ear splitting whistling and hooting from all the ships in the harbour, signalling that at long last the weary 1914-18 war was over. A loud whisper ran round the room, "The armistice! The armistice is signed!" Kirton rounded on the class in anger. "Quiet, there!" he shouted, glaring at the whisperers. There followed an immediate, almost shocked silence. To me he said gruffly, "Go on with your translation, John".

The author goes on to mention how this 'stoic' man on prize-day at the close of that academic year spoke so feelingly of the long roll of ex-pupils who had died in the war. He had little use for heroics:- he felt only the tragic waste of their young lives. *"However the public may see them", he said "they will always be for me my boys", 'and then broke down, unable to speak from grief.'*[145]

The names of the Anderson Educational Institute pupils killed during the Ancre are listed in a memorial. Originally in the Institute Building, it now resides in the new Anderson High School. It was unveiled on the last Friday of term, June 1919. *The pupils then remained standing while Rev. Arch. Macintyre read out the list of the gallant dead, and it was noticeable that not a few tears were shed by several teachers and pupils as some well known and well loved name was read.*[146]

These Institute boys of the Ancre included David Anderson, Joseph Anderson, George Groat, Laurence Halcrow, William Johnston, William Robertson, William Sinclair and George Spence.

This impact upon the Anderson Educational Institute alone was profound, with a school roll of an estimated 143 just prior to the war.[147] In comparison, the University of Aberdeen, a much larger institution, lost twelve of her students during the assault on Beaumont-Hamel.[148]

---

145   Anderson Educational Institute Centenary, booklet, ed., Graham John, (1962) p51. Shetland Museum and Archives, SA4/1303.

146   *Shetland News*, 3rd July, 1919.

147   Anderson Educational Institute School Log Book, 1899 - 1930, Shetland Museum and Archives. CO/5/7/3.

148   Cheyne, G.Y., *The Last Great Battle of the Somme, Beaumont-Hamel, 1916* (John Donald) 1988, p.28-29.

The local ministers gathered their thoughts. The Reverend Robert P. Fairlie spoke in the Lerwick Parish Church the following Sunday.

We remember them as youths of promise who had life been granted them should have accounted themselves great. But the measure of the span of a man's years is not the measure of his worth. For in that little that God has given them they have acquitted themselves like men and have fought the good fight. And while here we mourn their loss let us bear in mind those who in their homes today are in great grief and sorrow praying that God may grant them his gracious comfort.[149]

IN MEMORY OF W. R.

Killed at Beaumont Hamel, Nov. 13, 1916.

Flowers of past days,
Since 'that caresslike eve we strolled the way
Behind the lines that brood o'er stricken Serre,
Wind-driven now, as things that never were
Are widely blown afar. You might not stay
Once more to greet me, as we used to greet
Before the raw November dawn waked bright
In blood of men. Yet in that star-gemmed night,
When guns were hushed, your soul was mine to meet
As never theretofore. With the first ray
Of morning Fate had willed you should not stay.

Hushed guns that now are silenced evermore,
Old comrades who have sought the Great Far shore,
With all old things grow dim, The Y Ravine
Like formless dream recedes and fades away
With Beaumont Hamel, and that fearful day
When your fine soul fared west. Unheard, unseen,
Kind hours strew leaves upon the high desires
That died when you fell dead. But your great death
Brought forth a song as ne'er our mortal breath
Had cunning for. A song that re-inspires
Flowers of dead days.

S.

Poem in remembrance of William Robertson, 1st Battalion Gordon Highlanders, killed near Serre. The *Shetland Times*, 16th November, 1918.

---

149 *Shetland News*, 30th November, 1916.

The Reverend David Houston of St Olaf's Church mentioned:-

As a community we have been called on to render our share in young and valiant lives to the sacrifice demanded by this terrible war. They have made the sacrifice, but it has been made for every one of us, and we offer to the relatives of the glorious dead the homage of our admiration and sympathy. As a congregation we have contributed our part in George Groat, cut off, in the flower of his youth, the youngest of a brave and patriotic family, which has given five sons to the defence of the nation ... To these families and the immediately related, to us we offer our sincere, our poignant sympathy.[150]

That same day in Lerwick, in his sermon on Sunday forenoon, Reverend William Fotheringham at the Baptist Church equally transmitted the mood of the community:-

This has been a sad week for Lerwick, for our country, but more particularly the town. Sorrow had come home and knocked at our doors, but this sorrow is too deep, too near, and too sacred to speak of, and yet it would be less than just not to pay tribute to the sacrifice made by our neighbours and friends. To those who fell ... they shall live in our memory as brave men who fighting, fell forward as befits men. To those who suffer and sorrow, our Fellowship, we esteem them very highly for the sake of their sacrifice.[151]

The impact of the loss on the community was clear. However, the sentiment of the men who advanced towards the German lines that day should also be remembered in the midst of the local loss:-

Private William D Arthur:-
I must say that I am very sorry to see by the paper that so

---

150 *Shetland News*, 30th November, 1916.
151 *Shetland News*, 30th November, 1916.

many of the boys have fallen, and some of my best pals at that. I knew that we had lost heavily, but I did not know who had been killed, so I had been waiting very impatiently these last two weeks for the paper. How happy and cheerful every one of them was when they put on their armour and marched to the trenches, although we knew quite well that a lot of us would never come back. But who could tell who would be taken and who would be left? Any how, that never dampened our spirits, for we realised that at last we were going to get to grips with Fritz, for which we had been waiting for weeks.[152]

---

152 With the 'Terriers' on the Ancre, Interesting Narrative of the Big Push, *Shetland News*, 21st December, 1916.

FINAL THOUGHT

W e followed in our own granddad's footsteps, and that of the 51st Highland Division, on a family battlefield visit, and trips made since with school groups, and other interested parties. For a Shetlander – and any other - who makes a visit to the Somme battlefields, it would be a mistake not to make a point of visiting the Newfoundland Memorial Park. If you do go, please take this book with you to help remind you of their story.

The land itself was thankfully purchased in 1921 by the people of Newfoundland. In turn, it has been preserved and it is the largest battalion memorial on the Western Front. The Park is one of few sites on the Western Front where the ground remains largely untouched from when the First World War ended. The Park includes the area over which the Newfoundland Regiment made their unsuccessful attack on 1 July 1916 during the first day of the Somme, suffering atrocious losses.

At the northern tip of the Park, a flight of steps leads you up between two lions to the 51st Highland Division Memorial. There a kilted highlander holding a Lee Enfield rifle, gazes towards the German trenches in Y-Ravine, and the village of Beaumont-Hamel; all of which cost so much. A piece of ground in front marks where so many Shetlanders were killed and wounded. It was originally planned that the memorial be situated in the village of Beaumont-Hamel, but there were too many subterranean workings, dugouts, and tunnels to support the weight of the granite and bronze Memorial. In the village of Beaumont-Hamel itself there is the 51st Division Memorial Flagstaff, a simple yet poignant reminder of the cost of taking this small village on the 13th of November 1916.

The memorial was made from granite shipped from Aberdeenshire just after the war. It was carried by six carts and pulled by a team of horses and finally 'reconstructed' where it now stands, being unveiled on 28th September 1924 by Marshal

Y-Ravine, 7th Gordons attack location.

Photo: Jon Sandison

of France, Ferdinand Foch, former Allied Supreme Commander. On the front is a plaque inscribed in Gaelic:- *La Blair s'math n Cairdean - "Friends are good on the day of battle"*. Upon reading this, we thought how important friends would be on this day having been brought up in an isolated intertwined community like Shetland.

The battlefield of Beaumont-Hamel within the Newfoundland Memorial Park is, today, a relatively short walk over a small piece of ground. The casualties endured by the 51st Highland Division alone during the month of November came to over 2,000. It was

The author at the Beaumont-Hamel flagstaff that commemorates the capture of the village by the 51st (Highland) Division on 13 November 1916.

Photo: Jon Sandison

estimated that casualties during the Ancre represented 45 per cent of those who took part in the attack.[153] Testament to this loss is provided by the 51st Highland Memorial at Y-Ravine. Walking down towards the 7th Gordons assault position at Y-Ravine, you can look back up to see the Memorial. We were also aware that we were looking in the direction from which the Germans would have been defending as the 51st Highland Division attacked. The Highlanders would have been out of view until they came over the ridge. When their heads first started to appear over that top, German machine guns let rip. Looking at the memorial left vivid thoughts.

With the end of the Somme on 18th November 1916, the Shetland troops had played their part in taking Beaumont-Hamel. So many of them departed on the s.s. *Cambria*, on that Sunday evening back in June 1915, waving goodbye to loved ones. Disappearing, with the hope that a precious letter would get through either way, leaving families and friends behind. So many of them were side by side, local boys with whom they had grown up, as they went over the top on the Ancre. Most *did* come home from the war, and the Western Front. Many who survived went on to contribute to our community and elsewhere, but with unfathomable mental scars of what they had experienced. Most of the 22 were little more than twenty years old. Fresh faced, full of enthusiasm, with hope for the future and a world in front of them which none would live to see. A world that still witnesses conflict one hundred years on. All had already contributed so much to our community, lost in a snapshot of time. In the here and now, we can only look at their photos again, their names, pausing to contemplate their individual stories; each a person, a loved one, son, brother, boyfriend or a just a friend.

153 Bewsher, F.W., The *History of the Fifty First (Highland) Division* (William Blackwood and Sons) 1921, p.23

Marshal Foch delivering unveiling address for the 51st (Highland) Division Memorial, 28th September, 1924. Commemorating the recapture of the village by the Division, 13th November, 1916. Photograph courtesy of the Gordon Highlanders Museum

THE FALLEN

1st BATTALION GORDON HIGHLANDERS (SERRE)

Private David Anderson, aged 20, 13th November, Hoolsgarth, Albany Street, Lerwick. Queens Cemetery Puisuex.

Private Gilbert Brown, aged 20, 13th November, 15 Hangcliff Lane, Lerwick. Thiepval Memorial.

Private William Hughson, aged 23, 13th November, 7 Union Street, Lerwick. Serre Road Cemetery, No 1.

Private William Johnston, aged 20, 13th November, North Roadside, Lerwick. Euston Road Cemetery, Colincamps.

Private William Gilbert Manson, aged 20, 1st Battalion. Died from wounds on 1st January 1917, 35 Commercial Road, Lerwick. Boulogne Eastern Cemetery.

Private Arthur McCarthy, aged 23, 16th November, Customs House, Lerwick. Varennes Military Cemetery.

Corporal Laurence Bain Mackay, age 22, 13th November, 1st Battalion Gordon Highlanders, 57 Commercial Street, Lerwick. Queens Cemetery Puisieux.

Corporal William Robertson, aged 21, 13th November, 1st Battalion Gordon Highlanders, Askelon, Sullom, Northmavine. Queens Cemetery, Puisieux.

4TH AND 7TH BATTALION GORDON HIGHLANDERS (BEAUMONT-HAMEL)

Lance Corporal Magnus Christie, aged 19, 17th November, 1916. Skibhoull, Cunningsburgh. Thiepval Memorial.

Private Robert Coutts, aged 21, 14th November. 1 Pilot Lane, Lerwick. Varennes Military Cemetery.

Private David Evans, aged 26, 13th November, Customs House, Lerwick. Thiepval Memorial.

Private George Groat, aged 20, 13th November, Commercial Road, Lerwick. Thiepval Memorial.

Private Laurence Halcrow, aged 19, 13th November, 25 Burgh Road. Y-Ravine Cemetery.

Private John William Jamieson, aged 21, 13th November, Hamnavoe, Burra. Y-Ravine Cemetery.

Private William Kay, aged 24, 13th November, 47 Burgh Road, Lerwick. Thiepval Memorial.

Private Andrew Simpson, aged 22, 13th November, 19 St Magnus Street, Lerwick. Ancre Cemetery, Beaumont-Hamel.

Private James W Sinclair, aged 19, 13th November, 26 Albany Street, Lerwick. Thiepval Memorial.

Private Gilbert Smith, aged 33, died 26th November from wounds, Uyeasound, Unst. Wimereux Communal Cemetery.

Private George Spence, aged 21, 13th November, Nornagarth, Cullivoe, Yell. Ancre Cemetery, Beaumont-Hamel.

SPORTSMAN BATTALION, ROYAL FUSILIERS

Joseph Anderson, aged 24, 13th November, Lerwick. Canadian Cemetery No 2, Neuville St Vaast.

2nd BATTALION, ROYAL SCOTS

Robert William Inkster, aged 27, 13th November, Grangemouth, formerly Burra. Thiepval Memorial.

93rd FIELD AMBULANCE
ROYAL ARMY MEDICAL CORPS

Private George Stout, aged 28, 13th November, Edinburgh, formerly Busta, Fair Isle. Couin British Cemetery.

SOURCES AND ACKNOWLEDGEMENTS

This story could not be possible without the assistance, contributions and expertise of many people and sources. There are far too many to mention, but where possible they are listed below. To anyone I have missed, I apologise. If there are any mistakes, these will be entirely my own. However, a rewarding factor from research into the Shetland soldiers of the Great War is that each new discovery opens up a new avenue. Therefore any mistakes or omissions will always be seen in a positive light.

Thanks to our father Bruce Sandison for instilling a passion, fascination and continual desire to find out more about this story. Bruce is the son of Private William Andrew Sandison, Service No. 6386, Shetland Territorials, 7th Battalion Gordon Highlanders. He was in France from December 1915 until being wounded during the German offensive on 21st and 22nd of March 1918, at that time being awarded the Military Medal. He was nearly three years in France. The remainder of his war was spent with the 2nd Battalion Gordon Highlanders in Italy. After war, he spent time at the whaling. He was one of six Shetland pallbearers at the funeral of Ernest Shackleton at South Georgia, 1922.

Countless books have been written about the wider experience of the Great War, and the Somme. The work of both Lyn MacDonald, Martin Middlebrook, Denis Winter, and Peter Hart incorporate much of the experience as told by the soldiers themselves. Such accounts will continue to be even more valuable, with the passage of time. We do not have that luxury, apart from oral stories passed between each generation.

In his introduction to Robert Greig's memoir, the late Alex Cluness, provided a marvellous historiography of wider books available on the First World War.[1] In approaching this book, perhaps some less familiar books have been consulted to further examine the 'Scottish' experience. They include the works of Bewsher, and Falls, and more recently Campbell and French. All have a focus on the 51st Highland Division, and within that, the Gordon Highlanders.

PUBLISHED SOURCES

Anderson Educational Institute Centenary, ed., John Graham, (T.&J. Manson, 1962).

Anderson Educational Institute school log book (1899 - 1930). Shetland Museum and Archives CO/5/7/3

Anderson Educational Institute Roll of Honour.

Bewsher, F.W., The History of the Fifty First (Highland) Division (William Blackwood & Sons, 1921.)

Campbell, C., Engine of Destruction, (Argyll Publishing, 2013).

Campbell, Colin & Green, Rosalind, Can't Shoot a Man with a Cold. Lt. E. Alan Mackintosh, M.C., 1893-1917. Poet of the Highland Division (Argyll Publishing, 2004).

Cave, Nigel, Somme:- Beaumont Hamel, Newfoundland Park (Pen and Sword Books, 2010).

Cheyne, G.Y., The Last Great Battle of the Somme, Beaumont Hamel, 1916 (John Donald Publishers, 1988)

Churchill, Winston S. The World Crisis, Vol III, 1916-1918 (Bloomsbury, 1950).

Duffy, Christopher, Through German Eyes, The British and The Somme, 1916 (Phoenix, 2006)

French, C., Friends Are Good on The Day of Battle (Helion & Company Ltd., 2017).

Falls, Cyril, Life of a Regiment, Vol IV, Official History of the Gordon Highlanders (Aberdeen University Press, 1958).

---

1 Greig, R. M., ed., Alex Cluness, *Doing His Bit. A Shetland Soldier in the Great War* (Shetland Times), Lerwick, 1999, p.xii - xiii.

Greig, R.M., ed. Alex Cluness, Doing His Bit. A Shetland Soldier in the Great War (Shetland Times, 1999).

Holmes, Richard, The Western Front (Ebury Publishing, 1999).

Holmes, Richard, Tommy. The British Soldier On The Western Front (Harper Collins Publishers, 2004).

Manson, Thomas, ed., Shetland's Roll of Honour and Service (T.&J. Manson, 1920)

Macdonald, Lyn, Somme (Penguin Books, 1983).

Mitchinson, K.W., England's Last Hope (Palgrave Macmillan, 1988).

Mitchinson, William, The Territorial Force at War, 1914-16 (Palgrave Macmillan, 2014)

Pottinger, James diary transcript, Shetland Museum and Archives, D1/452.

Prior, Robin and Wilson, Trevor, The Somme (Yale University Press, 2005).

Rorie, D., A Medico's Luck in the War (Naval and Military Press reprint, 1929).

Ross, Robert B., The Fifty-First in France (Naval and Military History Press, 1918).

Riddell, Linda K., Shetland and the Great War (Shetland Times, 2015).

Sandison, Dr R., A Family At War 1914-1918 (Shetland Life) November 1996.

Shelden, Jack, The German Army On The Somme, 1914-1916 (Pen & Sword, 2012).

Sheffield, G., The Somme (Cassell Military Paperbacks, 2003).

Simkins, P., Kitchener's Army. The Raising of The New Armies, 1914-16 (Manchester University Press, 1988).

Simkins, P., From The Somme to Victory (Pen and Sword Books, 2014)

Taylor, A.J.P., The First World War (Penguin, 1966).

Whittingham, D., Mud in The Great War:- Myth and Memory (Hambledon, 2005).

ARCHIVAL SOURCES

1st Battalion War Diary Gordon Highlanders, National Archives WO95/1435 .

2nd Battalion Royal Scots, War Diary, National Archives WO95/1423/3 .

4th Battalion Gordon Highlanders, War Diary, National Archives WO95/2880/4

7th Battalion War Diary, Gordon Highlanders, National Archives WO95/288/2 .

Robert Inkster service record, National Archives WO/363.

Shetland Times and Shetland News, November and December, 1916.

Scottish Naturalist (Edinburgh, Oliver & Boyd), No 61, January, 1917.

Battle of the Ancre. Troops outside a London coffee stall at Auchonvillers, a starting-point of the British attacks on Beaumont-Hamel. November 1916.

Photograph courtesy: Imperial War Museum

The late Alex Cluness; Angus Johnson and Blair Bruce, Shetland Archives; Chris Baker:- Long Long Trail; Chris McDonald and Carolyn Morrisey; Colin Campbell; Derek Bird, Western Front Association, Northern Branch; Dr Ian Tait, Shetland Museum and Archives; Dr Linda Riddell; Commonwealth War Graves Commission; Elizabeth Angus and Kate Canter, Shetland Family History Society; George Jamieson; Gordon Highlanders Museum (Bert Innes, Charles Reid and Ruth Duncan); Imperial War Museum; James Mainland; John Sandison; Jenny Murray and Laurie Goodlad, Shetland Museum and Archives; Margaret Cooper - William Robertson diary; Martin Emslie - James Houston diary; Michelle Henderson. George Stout notes; Ray Urwen, Laurence Bain Mackay notes; Stuart Robertson, David Anderson Notes, William Mitchinson.

Overall, enormous gratitude must be shown to Karen Fraser, Shetland Library and staff at Shetland Archives whose continued support and encouragement made this publication possible, alongside the funding granted for the project from the Scottish Government Public Library Improvement Fund.

Finally, and most of all, thanks to my much better half Louise, and our own "Shetland son" Findlay, for their continued patience, support and tolerance with my seemingly never ending obsession of the Shetland soldiers of the Great War.

The men of 1914-18 are not forgotten.

IN MEMORIAM

From Home:
To the Men Who Fell at Beaumont-Hamel

The pale sun woke in the eastern sky
And a veil of moist was drawn
Over the faces of death and fame
When you went up in the dawn.
With never a thought of death or fame,
Only the work to do,
When you went over the top, my friends,
And I not there with you.

Lt. E. Alan Mackintosh M.C. 1893-1917.
Poet of Highland Division (killed at Cambrai, 1917).[1]

---

1   Campbell, Colin & Green, Rosalind, *Can't Shoot a Man with a Cold. Lt. E. Alan Mackintosh,*
     MC, 1893-1917. Poet of the Highland Division (Argyll Publishing), 2004 p.164.

51st (Highland) Division Memorial, Beaumont-Hamel, Somme.

Photo: Jon Sandison

1. William Johnston

6. William Manson

11. Arthur McCarthy

2. William Kay

7. David Anderson

12. Gilbert Brown

3. Laurence Halcrow

8. David Evans

13. Robert Coutts

4. William Hughson

9. James Sinclair

14. Joseph Anderson

5. Andrew Simpson

10. George Mackay

15. Laurence Mackay

SECOND EDIT

North Loch

LOCH OF CLICKHIMIN

ZETLAND SHEET LIII. 13.

1901

Lerwick fatalities at
Battle of the Ancre,
November 1916